What the Pros Are Saying About Peak Performance Golf

"I've worked with Dr. Patrick J. Cohn since turning professional in 1988 and have found his practice strategies and mental preparation techniques to be very helpful in my career. He's taught me how to practice with a purpose and a mission, and how to play good golf without worrying about perfect mechanics. This book will show you how to practice using your imagination, feel, and instincts rather than striving for mechanical perfection."

—*Brian Watts, PGA Tour, 12-time winner on the Japanese Tour*

"To play well every week, you have to practice and prepare your best on and off the golf course. In *Peak Performance Golf*, Dr. Patrick Cohn helps golfers do just this. And with his help, I have a more balanced practice plan, which has allowed me to play my best every week."

—*Frank Lickliter, PGA Tour*

"*Peak Performance Golf* is the best book on the market for helping you become tournament ready. I've learned that to play well, you have to know you will play well before going to the first tee. Dr. Cohn has helped me get into a confident state of mind by focusing on success instead of past failure."

—*Glen Hnatiuk, PGA Tour*

"To win at any level, you have to train both your mind and body. Dr. Cohn does an excellent job of teaching you how to develop confidence and touch around the greens in *Peak Performance Golf*, which are vital to any player's success. Dr. Cohn has taught me excellent practice drills for putting that have helped me become a better putter."

—*J. L. Lewis,* PGA *Tour winner*

PEAK PERFORMANCE GOLF

How Good Golfers Become Great Ones

Patrick Cohn, Ph.D.

CB

CONTEMPORARY BOOKS

Library of Congress Cataloging-in-Publication Data

Cohn, Patrick J., 1960–
    Peak performance golf : how good golfers become great ones /
Patrick J. Cohn.
      p.   cm.
    Includes bibliographical references and index.
    ISBN 0-8092-2432-1
    1. Golf—Training.   I. Title.
    GV979.T68C65   2000
    796.352'3—dc21   99-40995
                                                CIP

Cover design by Nick Panos
Cover photograph copyright © Pete Turner/Image Bank
Interior design by Precision Graphics
Interior photographs by Joe Brooks Photography, Orlando, FL

Published by Contemporary Books
A division of NTC/Contemporary Publishing Group, Inc.
4255 West Touhy Avenue, Lincolnwood (Chicago), Illinois 60712-1975 U. S. A.
Copyright © 2000 by Patrick Cohn
Printed in the United States of America
International Standard Book Number: 0-8092-2432-1

00 01 02 03 04 05 VH .19 18 17 16 15 14 13 12 11 10 9 8 7 6 5 4 ·3 2

CONTENTS

FOREWORD

Players on the professional tours are blessed with physical talent, but talent alone doesn't make a champion golfer. Some golfers have more physical ability than others, but successful tour players have refined their God-given talent with years of purposeful practice.

I know you, too, have golf ability, but you can't reach your potential without developing that skill through practice and instruction, just like the pros. It doesn't matter if you have only 1 hour a week or as many as 40 hours a week to work on your game; to get the most out of your practice, it needs to be quality, focused practice. My friend and mental coach, Dr. Patrick Cohn, shows you a great system to help lay out a practice plan to play your best golf.

When I played golf for Oklahoma State University in the mid- to late 1980s, not many players engaged in mental training, fitness, diet, or injury prevention techniques. I was more into beating balls and gaining experience as a player. But I've seen a lot of important changes in golf instruction and player development in the last 15 years. Playing with some of the best players in the world on the Japan, Nike, and PGA tours for the last 10 years, I've learned how to be a complete player, top to bottom. Years ago no one worked with a specialist, but today most every player I know works closely with a golf instructor, stays physically fit, watches his or her diet, and consults with a sports psychologist or physical therapist. I now know how vital all these areas are to any player's success. You, too, will be a more complete player if you take advantage of the resources available to improve your game, starting with Dr. Cohn's peak performance training program.

Your game will improve at a faster rate when you follow a specific practice routine and commit to improving every day and every week. If you want to win your first club championship or a U.S.

Open or just want to play better on weekends, you should do everything possible to prepare, both on and off the golf course. Besides getting the best instruction you can and training your mind and body off the course, you should develop a plan to prepare for tournaments. This means playing a practice round, learning the golf course, and mapping out a strategy to play each hole. And when you do practice on the range, don't just beat golf balls. Practice the predominate shots you'll face on the course that week. If the course setup requires you to hit a lot of long irons, for example, practicing long irons should be a priority.

Dr. Cohn also shows you how to set daily, short-term, and long-term goals, which are instrumental for any player's success. I've learned that you should shoot for the stars and set lofty goals for your game. Yet make your goals attainable, so you can develop confidence as you progress and reach each one. Good luck in your golf pursuits, and I hope you enjoy reading *Peak Performance Golf*.

—**Brian Watts,** PGA *Tour player and winner of 12 PGA Japanese Tour events*

ACKNOWLEDGMENTS

This project could not have been completed without the help of three dedicated colleagues. I want to thank Mike Bender, PGA professional, Paul Geisler, M.A., ATC/L, and Karen Beerbower, M.S., R.D., for contributing their expertise to *Peak Performance Golf* and for their professionalism in this endeavor. I very much appreciate the valuable input during the writing process of colleagues James Walker, Edward Travis, and Chris Hallead. I also want to thank the editorial staff of NTC/Contemporary Publishing Group, Inc., for copyediting and polishing the manuscript. Lastly, I want to thank every golfer, professional and amateur, who has shared his or her views on effective practice and preparation for winning golf.

INTRODUCTION

In today's hi-tech and competitive world, golfers are bigger, stronger, better equipped, and better trained. To keep up with the competition, a player must stay on top of advances in performance enhancement. To reach peak performance, golfers must engage in a holistic training program that includes golf-specific training and practice regimens. If you are not taking advantage of advances in golf instruction, sports psychology, physical therapy, nutrition, and exercise science, your competitors are passing you by. PGA Tour star Tiger Woods is a good example of how a comprehensive training program that includes swing mechanics, sports psychology, physical therapy, and exercise science can help someone become a dominant player in golf. Starting at an early age with the guidance of his father, Tiger trained and prepared in every facet of his game. He worked with a PGA instructor, sports psychologist, athletic trainer, physical therapist, and equipment specialists.

Today, more and more golfers are exercising regularly, seeking nutritional guidance, and working with physical therapists and sports psychologists. *Peak Performance Golf* describes a comprehensive training and preparation program for serious golfers who want to see how good they can become. This total training program draws expertise from several disciplines to help you get more out of practice, train better, learn faster, and thus perform better. Expert advice in the fields of golf instruction, golf psychology, motor learning and performance, physical therapy and exercise science, and nutrition are brought together in this book to give you the latest golf-specific training techniques. A complete training program that integrates these disciplines is necessary to stay competitive with players who are practicing more efficiently and are stronger, more fit, mentally tougher, and smarter.

The game of golf presents demands unlike those of any other sport. The mental, physical, and strategic challenges of the game make it both fun and frustrating. You can go only so far with physical talent. To reach one's potential, one's talent must be refined and polished. The best golfers in the world, such as Greg Norman, Tiger Woods, and David Duval, have tremendous talent, but they have combined their abilities with hard work, hours of practice, and mental discipline. They practice to win. These great players know how to train and prepare themselves to get the most out of their physical ability. I decided to write *Peak Performance Golf* to give golfers a better understanding of what affects their performance and how they can best prepare themselves for competition.

Perhaps because golf is one of the most complex and difficult games you can play, players are constantly bombarded with information on the golf swing, equipment, putting stroke, mental game, and course strategies. Every teacher, club manufacturer, and physical trainer has his own philosophy and methodology. What expert should you listen to? The golf world is filled with differing philosophies about how to play and how to teach the game. You can read about it in books and magazines, see it on the Golf Channel, hear it on the radio, find it on the Internet, and get it from your local teaching professional. The challenge is to untangle all the information and uncover what's right for *you*. How do you know what's right for your game? The best way is to find a teacher who talks in your language, communicates well, and has a solid philosophy for teaching the golf swing. In this book, you will learn how to pick an instructor who is right for you and how to better apply each lesson to your game.

Second, golfers must play on a variety of courses and in various conditions, which demands specialized training and practice. In many other sports, such as bowling, the player competes under similar conditions from day to day—the size and length of bowling alleys, for example, and environmental conditions stay constant. A bowler doesn't have to contend with uneven lies, wind, rain, or hazards, as golfers do. Every time you tee the ball up, it's a new experience with new challenges. Every shot you hit is unique. You play 18 different holes with various terrains, yardage, shape, and look. Wind, temperature, and moisture can drastically change how you play a course from one day to the next. Because of these factors, golfers must prepare and practice in a highly specialized manner. In this book you will learn how to structure your practice to perform well in any situation you encounter on the course.

Third, playing golf day in and day out tests the durability of the human body. Many experts agree that the golf swing places tremendous stress on the body. The spine, back muscles, and upper-extremity joints can become strained from daily practice and play. The twisting and rotating action of the golf swing can result in spine, back, or shoulder injuries. Great players such as Fred Couples, Davis Love III, Greg Norman, and several others have been forced to take time off to recover from golf injuries. Lack of physical conditioning, swing faults, and poor posture in the setup can open the door to a variety of physical injuries. Many golfers don't warm up properly before they play, which can lead to a muscle pull or strain, or aggravate an existing injury.

To become good at golf, one must practice a lot. And when a player practices or plays every day, as many touring pros do, overuse injuries like tennis elbow are common side effects. Thus, a big challenge for golfers is to stay in good physical condition and avoid career-ending injuries. This book will show you how to avoid the most common injuries that plague golfers.

Fourth, playing golf taxes one's physical endurance. A four-hour round can tire even the most fit golfer. Therefore, physical fitness is becoming a regular part of professional and amateur golfers' daily routines. Today, tour pros are working out more than ever before. All the major tours have on-site fitness trailers specifically designed to provide players with exercise and physical therapy.

Fifth, playing golf challenges your mental makeup. It's just you against the golf course. Golf is a solitary pursuit. You take all the glory for sinking a 30-footer and you take the blame for hitting a ball in the water. Golf is also challenging because it's a self-paced sport. In most sports, play is continuous, with occasional time-outs and breaks between periods. But in golf, one must be able to focus for hours and to turn one's focus on and off with each shot. The golfer has too much time to think about each shot, analyze the situation, and overprepare for the shot. Overanalysis, doubt, and indecision are often a golfer's toughest opponents. In *Peak Performance Golf*, you will learn how to integrate mental skills into your regular practice routines so you can be mentally prepared to play your best.

Sixth, long hours on the course coupled with the mental and physical demands of the game require that players meet certain basic nutritional requirements. Most golfers overlook better nutrition as a means of enhancing performance. I don't recommend that you eat volcanic ash, as Jesper Parnevik, but I believe in the idea "you are what you eat." A balanced diet can have profound effects on many areas of a golfer's game. Proper nutrition increases your energy and endurance: you don't want to get to the 15th tee and run out of fuel for your body. Good nutrition that maintains high energy levels can also enhance your ability to concentrate. Without proper nutrients, minerals, and the right combination of protein, carbohydrate, and fat, your body and mind cannot function at peak efficiency. In addition, eating the right foods at the right time can improve your confidence and self-image.

Last, an area that is neglected by many golf instructors and much golf literature is course management. Any good player can hit a great shot to a flag in the range, when it doesn't count. Conversely, the strategic challenges of golf can make the best ballstrikers look like high-handicap players. The game of golf is played primarily between your ears. How well you keep the ball in play and score reflects your ability to strategically manage your game. You can't win without this ability. In this book I present a system for playing smart golf by studying the course and setting up a game plan for each round you play.

Most players do not know the best training methods to meet the challenges of golf. Hitting balls without a specific purpose on the practice range does not translate readily to playing a shot with creativity and imagination on the golf course. Honing your swing on the range is only a small part of what it takes to win at any level of golf. Swinging great on the range is not what makes a great player. If you want to win at golf, you must train, prepare, and practice as a winner does.

To compete and win, golfers today must stay physically healthy, avoid injury, have sound mechanics, be mentally tough, eat right, and practice efficiently. These elements of the game are the focus of *Peak Performance Golf*. True, you can probably improve your game by doing it your way and without the help of experts. But if you read this book with an open mind, I think you can improve without spending more time practicing than you do now. This book will teach you how to prepare like a pro. If you are a pro, the advice included here will help you reach your peak by showing you how to train for strength, endurance, flexibility, fitness, and avoidance of injury. I'll show you how to better apply your practice to tournament play, and how to play smart, strategic golf. I'll also give you the low-down on mental preparation and how to synthesize it into your regular practice routine.

Serious golfers are on a mission to play great golf. Do you have a mission and do you know how to practice and prepare to help you be successful in this mission? Most players don't have a training plan or even a set of goals, but many are getting on the bandwagon. *Peak Performance Golf* describes a multidisciplined approach to training and preparation for tournament golf. If your goal is to get a leg up on the competition, this book will give you an important piece of the puzzle of peak performance. Let's get started!

I would like to identify other writers' contributions to *Peak Performance Golf*. Mike Bender was my main source for writing Chapter Three on getting more out of your golf instruction. He is a *GOLF Magazine* top 100 teacher and director of instruction at Timacuan Golf Academy in Orlando, Florida. Paul Geisler, M.A., ATC/L, helped me write Chapters Six and Seven on fitness for golf and injury prevention. Paul is president of KineticGolf and SPEC Systems, Inc. and a biomechanics instructor in the Department of Health and Kinesiology at Georgia Southern University in Statesboro, Georgia. Karen Sue Beerbower, M.S., R.D., was my main source for writing Chapter Eight on nutrition for golf. Karen is the president of Nutritional Guidance, Inc., in Winter Park, Florida.

CHAPTER ONE

FINDING YOUR MISSION

All great athletes, such as Tiger Woods, Ken Griffey, Jr., and Brett Favre, have a desire to be great in their sport. What fuels their desire or motivation to be the best? Where do their determination, desire, and motivation come from? How much of these qualities fuel their success? We know that talent alone is not enough for success. These athletes are successful because of a combination of physical talent, desire, mental toughness, knowledge about their sport, and determination to be the best. Do great athletes strive for success more than other, less successful athletes do? I think so. And where do they get this high motivation to succeed?

Motivation to excel in a sport starts with a person's dream or mission. For many golfers, this dream begins early in life when they caddy for a parent and fall in love with the game. Others realize early in life that they have enough talent and potential to be a great player, and they engross themselves in the mission to be the best they can be.

The best golfers in the world have an intense desire to be great, which is fueled by their childhood dreams of winning their first junior tournament, becoming a club champion, winning a college tournament, or winning the U.S. Open. Childhood dreams fuel the drive to practice and play day after day and learn as much as possible about the game.

But motivation only starts with a dream. Great players like Greg Norman, Tiger Woods, and Ernie Els do more than just dream about being great, because it's not enough just to fantasize about playing great golf. A player's dreams will go unfulfilled without desire and energy. Your dream is the spark that starts the fire inside you. It is your responsibility to feed the fire to help your dreams become real.

THE SEVEN KEYS TO A MISSION

Motivation is important to success in any endeavor—it is the drive to reach a goal, to become better, to practice day after day, or to be the best one can be. What is motivation, and what does it take to become highly motivated? It encompasses several components, or building blocks, which a player must embrace to reach greatness. These building blocks, which I refer to collectively as your "mission," include the following:

1. a dream of where you want to go or achieve
2. a vision of how to work toward the dream
3. the desire to carry out the vision
4. the power to do what it takes day to day
5. the guidance to know and do what is right
6. the wisdom to believe you are on the right path
7. the determination to overcome obstacles in your path

For any athlete, motivation starts within the player's imagination. The athlete's dreams start a fire inside to accomplish something great and fulfill whatever the dream may be. Different players have different dreams—to break 80, to be club champion, to win the U.S. Amateur, or to win the U.S. Open. The building blocks of a mission are similar to those a builder uses to construct a house. The golfer's motivation, just like the builder's, starts within the imagination.

There are two types of dreamers in the world. The first is the daydreamer. The daydreamer fantasizes about what it would be like to be the next Michael Jordan or Greg Norman. The daydreamer engages in wishful thinking, never taking steps to realize the dream. The daydreamer's dreams are delusions, because he does not have the desire or commitment to make the dream a reality.

The second type of dreamer is the visionary. The visionary dreams of great accomplishments and is motivated to act on his dream. No accomplishment is impossible for the visionary dreamer. The visionary has the inner desire and power to strive for his goals.

> *We've removed the ceiling above our dreams.*
> *There are no more impossible dreams.*
>
> —*Jesse Jackson*

From dreams flow the rest of your mission. A mission is more than a vision; it's also a plan—a plan of the path you will take to get to where you want to go. Once a builder dreams, or "imagines," the house he wants to build, he works with an architect to devise a working plan of the house. The dream provides purpose and the vision provides understanding of how to build the dream. The builder has an idea and a plan, but construction has not begun. The builder needs know-how and desire to carry out the plan. Without know-how and desire, the architect's plan is just a drawing on paper. The plan is meaningless until the builder has the desire to implement the plan. Similarly, a golfer can have a great plan, but he must first have the commitment to carry out the plan on a day-to-day basis.

Once the commitment is present, an athlete must have the power to do what it takes to become the best he can be. This is the point at which the athlete moves from imagination to action. He must have the energy to do the day-to-day grind necessary for growth. Using the analogy of the builder, we can say the plan is in action and the building process has begun. Now the builder uses his resources and energy to hire the contractors and oversee the construction.

The next building block of a mission is guidance. Desire and energy are useless without the tools and skills needed to execute your plan, and these tools and skills are acquired through the guidance of others. No world-class golfer is self-taught in the truest sense. Everyone, even talented golfers such as Tiger Woods, receives help along the way from his teacher, family, and friends. Ben Crenshaw attributed his win at the 1995 Masters to the early lessons he learned from the late Harvey Penick.

In today's world, finding golf guidance is so easy that it can almost be overwhelming. You can take lessons from numerous instructors. You can read an array of instructional books. This is where the sixth building block of your mission—wisdom—comes in. You have a dream, a plan to achieve the dream, the desire and energy to act, and the support of instructors and other people along the way. Now the critical component of your mission is the wisdom to choose your method and trust in the people who advise and instruct you along the way. Many players come to work with me after having jumped from one instructor to another, complaining that no one has helped them play better. These golfers can't commit to one instructor or method and thus are constantly searching for a magic fix. I discuss how to hook up with an instructor who is right for you and how to get the most out of each lesson.

As you work toward your dream and put faith in the people who guide you, you need the determination to stick to your plan and stay on your mission. This is what will get you back on track when adversity hits, what lifts you back on the horse when you get thrown off. Determination helps you recover from temporary setbacks and keeps you working day after day during those times that you seem to be spinning your wheels. When you fail—and everyone experiences failure along the way—determination is what helps you to pick up the pieces and make the necessary changes in your game. When I think of determination, I think of Greg Norman. His determination to bounce back from setbacks is stronger than most. And that is the mark of a champion.

MAKE IT *YOUR* MISSION

You should identify what you plan to accomplish and how you see yourself as you go after it. Remember that this must be *your* mission and not the expectations others have for you. If you decide to try to satisfy your parents, friends, or coaches, rather than be truly self-motivated, you won't enjoy the process along the way. With this type of motivation, you will most likely question why you are doing what you are doing. You may lose the desire and energy to carry out your plan. Dreams and visions come from inside you; other people in your life throw demands and expectations upon you.

Sometimes parents push a child into playing a sport they once played, often for their own vicarious gratification. Parents want the best for their children, but what parents think is the best is not always the same as what a child finds enjoyable. And, as a rule, children want to please their parents. So it's common for a child to accept a parent's dream as his own.

COMMITTING TO YOUR MISSION

Not only do great players have a dream, they dream about achieving their goals. Commitment is what separates players who have a dream from those who live their dream. Imagine that you are at the end of your golfing career and are looking back at your life. What would you like to be able to say about your golf career? Did you reach your goals? How would you like others to see you?

Your commitment to stick to your dream is even more critical when people close to you question how realistic your dream is. Commitment is tested when others say to you, "Why do you spend so much time playing golf? You will never be a good player." I work with many mini-tour pros who battle pressure from parents and friends to give up their dream. The pressure from others to "get a real job" can make players question their mission. If others derail you and your aspirations, that can erode your dream—but only if you internalize and buy into their view. A struggling player has a choice: he can let others destroy his confidence, or he can use their opinions to deepen his commitment and desire.

The willpower to stick to your dream in the face of failure is also important. Slumps, injury, and failure can test the resolve of even the best golfers. Many players have given up on their dreams after trying to overcome a slump or injury. Most likely a player starts to question his goals when his confidence is low. Your vision may be tested when you start to question your own ability and wonder if you can achieve your goals. This is when you have to recommit yourself to your dream and remember why you play the game. My advice is this: never give up your dream, because it's the process of striving for your dreams that makes life interesting and enjoyable.

In the following chapter, you will learn how to evolve your dreams into a specific mission. This mission will become the foundation of your practice plan—a plan that defines what you need to do to become the very best you can be.

CHAPTER TWO

GETTING STARTED WITH YOUR TOTAL TRAINING PROGRAM

Golfers need more than physical talent, the right equipment, and a well-tuned swing to keep up with the competition. Today we have new frontiers in performance enhancement for golf, including the application of sports psychology, motor learning, physical therapy, exercise science, and nutrition. These are the newest tools that coaches use to help athletes get the most out of their physical ability, and that motivated golfers use to reach peak performance. Along with recent technological improvements in equipment, our knowledge of performance enhancement has also grown. In fact, our understanding of nutrition, physical conditioning, and sports psychology helped Olympic athletes set new world records during the 1996 Olympic Games in Atlanta.

Athletes today need to take a multidimensional approach to training and overall preparation to both keep up with the competition and play their best. Many athletes are taking advantage of new training methods to get an edge on the competition. Nutritionists, physical therapists, biomechanic specialists, and sports psychologists are now considered a regular part of an athlete's training team. PGA Tour players do more than just train their golf swing. They understand the importance of fitness, nutrition, injury prevention, and mental training to reaching their peak and maintaining high levels of performance.

On the PGA Tour, many players seek the guidance of performance experts in several fields. Each player has a "support team" to address his physical, mental, nutritional, and biomechanical needs. An instructor gives advice on the golf swing. A sports psychologist teaches the mental game. A physical therapist treats injuries and improves fitness. A nutritionist prescribes a sound diet. All of these areas—the golf swing, the mental game, fitness level, and nutritional habits—are interrelated and dependent on each other.

This chapter outlines your training needs and gives you the tools to start a total training plan. The plan includes eight specific areas of "preparedness" in which every serious golfer needs to become involved. I believe this type of plan is the future of high-level training. In the following pages, you will learn exactly what a total training program involves, how to set a plan of action for training, and how to combine several training disciplines into your total training program. You will acquire the skills to put your plan to work on a daily basis and start working toward your dream.

TRAINING TO WIN

I know you already work very hard to improve your game, or you wouldn't be reading this book now. But compare your current training program to the eight parts of a total practice plan outlined below. A total practice plan should incorporate not only all of the disciplines mentioned in the opening paragraphs of this chapter, but also the areas of a total practice plan outlined here, each of which is discussed in detail in later chapters. To get an edge on the competition, you need to heed the advice of experts in these areas of training and preparation. One weak link in any of these areas can leave you unprepared to compete.

For you to play your best golf at the end of a training program, the program should include the eight elements described in the following pages.

1. INSTRUCTION THAT'S RIGHT FOR YOU

Good swing fundamentals are important to good golf. All PGA Tour players receive instruction from their swing coaches frequently. You need another set of eyes to give you objective feedback. In Chapter Three, I discuss how to find the best instructors. Instructors use different styles in teaching the golf swing, some of which may be more suited to your style of learning than others. Every teacher also has a unique philosophy of teaching the golf swing. An instructor must be able to communicate in a way that you can understand, or else you will not learn.

Once you begin taking lessons, the fun begins. In Chapter Three, I also discuss how to get the most out of your lessons. How much you learn and improve depends on your ability to integrate the lessons into practice. Learning occurs only with practice, but it should be the right type of practice. Practice must include training aids and tools that tell you whether you are practicing correctly.

Finally, you should develop a schedule for your instruction. At first the instruction may be as frequent as once a week. Later, you and your instructor might meet once a month to chart your progress. You will need to identify what changes you must make in your game, decide on a weekly schedule for practicing, and determine how much time you will devote to each area.

Your instructor should include all facets of the game—full swing, putting, chipping, wedge play, and bunker work—in his teaching. Don't neglect the most important parts of the game— putting and chipping, which accounts for more than half of the scoring in golf. A good short game can bail you out on those days when your ballstriking is not up to par. For example, if you don't hit a lot of greens, a good short game is essential if you want to get the ball up and down. And great putting is what wins tournaments.

The ultimate purpose of practice is to acquire a consistent swing that is right for you—not a perfect swing. The aim is *repeatability*. If pretty golf swings won tournaments, then players such as Steve Elkington would win every week on the PGA Tour, but they don't. The ability to repeat a swing under pressure, manage yourself around the course, and stay composed are the keys to winning. Too many golfers get consumed with trying to swing like, say, Ernie Els when they don't have his ability, size, or body type. Your swing should accord with your ability, size, and body type.

2. FOCUSED AND SPECIFIC PRACTICE

The second key area of training and preparation is practice habits. How you practice is crucial to getting the results you desire. Just going to the golf course and spending an hour on the range is not quality practice. Most golfers don't know how to practice efficiently. They don't understand the principles of learning and performance. If you practice the wrong way or work on the wrong things, you form bad habits. You can spend your whole day at the golf course beating balls and hitting putt after putt, but if you practice the wrong way, you are not learning or improving.

Getting the most out of your practice is critical. What does it mean to get the most out of your practice? It means the ability to enhance learning through sound principles of practice so that you can play your best once you step onto the course. Remember, the goal of practice and your total training program is to help you score better on the course. Effective practice includes:

1. learning how to take your practice game to the golf course
2. working on the mental game as you practice the physical game
3. using your practice time for focused, quality practice
4. understanding the principles of learning and how to accelerate the learning process
5. setting goals to improve swing technique, mental toughness, physical fitness, and health

In Chapter Four, I discuss in detail how to get the most out of your practice. For now, remember that practice does not make perfect unless it is focused practice!

3. MENTAL PREPARATION FOR TOURNAMENTS

The mental side of the game becomes more and more important as you learn the fundamentals of the golf swing and your swing becomes more consistent. Golfers often overlook the mental game because teachers and coaches don't stress the importance of focus, confidence, and trust in their instruction.

Also, there is a misconception that you can't train your mind while working on the physical part of the game. Many golfers separate the mental and physical parts of the game. I often hear players say, "I'll work on the mental side when I finish working on my swing." This approach ignores the fact that the mental game can easily be learned at the same time you are developing your physical game. For me, it's hard to separate the mental from the physical in golf. I don't care if you are as talented as Greg Norman—if your mind gets in the way of performance, you won't play up to your ability.

Here are five mental-game areas to incorporate into your practice plan, all of which are critical for improving your game:

1. improving your focus in practice
2. gaining confidence via practice
3. learning to control emotions in practice
4. practicing a playing mind-set
5. developing a preshot routine

A tremendous source of confidence is practice—the right kind of practice. Knowing that you are doing your best to integrate mental training, physical fitness, and good nutrition into your golf game will help to increase your overall confidence.

Sports psychology books are another great resource for learning about the mental game and applying it to your game. You can start by reading my first two books, *The Mental Game of Golf: A Guide to Peak Performance* and *The Mental Art of Putting: Using Your Mind to Putt Your Best*. Ideally, to improve your mental game, you should work with a sports psychologist one-on-one. Although it can be more expensive, this approach is much more effective, because each player has unique needs. Try to find a qualified sports psychologist who specializes in working with golfers.

4. Getting Fit for Golf

Today on the PGA, LPGA, and Senior tours, players are taking advantage of on-site fitness trailers and local health clubs to improve their overall health and stay in excellent physical condition. Some people argue that golf is not a "physical sport" and that athletic attributes such as strength and endurance are not necessary for playing good golf. But we know this is not the case. Physical fitness measures, including muscular strength, flexibility, cardiovascular fitness, and endurance, are just as important for golfers as they are for other athletes—and in some cases more important.

A physical fitness program should be a part of your regular practice routine, but it's best if it is also incorporated into your lifestyle. Maintaining physical fitness is great for your golf game, but it's good for you in other ways as well. Among the benefits of a regular exercise program are a reduced risk of cardiovascular disease, increased energy, improved mood state, and lower levels of stress.

But let's not overlook the many benefits that a regular exercise program will bring to your golf game. One is enhanced energy. If you are not in good physical condition, it's easy for you to run out of energy at the end of a round. A second advantage of regular exercise is increased muscular strength. Increasing strength helps you hit the ball farther with less effort. A third advantage is improved flexibility. Flexibility prevents injuries and helps you make a full, fluid swing unimpeded by tight muscles, which is especially important for senior golfers.

In short, the three main objectives of an exercise program are improved cardiovascular fitness, improved flexibility, and increased strength and stamina. In Chapter Five, I show you how to get started with a golf-specific exercise program and improve in these three areas. Getting started with an exercise program is easy; sticking with it is the hard part. More than half of all persons who start such a program drop it within a few weeks. So your commitment to working out is just as important as what you do when you work out.

Regular exercise can also improve your mental game. Your concentration improves when you have more energy at the end of a round. Exercise also helps to relax the body and quiet the mind. Natural endorphins are released during exercise and these hormones help calm you. Exercise also helps protect you from the adverse effects of stress and anxiety; it not only reduces stress, it helps you focus better under pressure.

5. Preventing Injuries and Staying Healthy

Even if you are in tiptop shape and are injury-free, a physical therapist or personal trainer is vital for helping you prevent injury or recover from an existing injury. The golf swing is not a natural motion: the stress placed on the spine, lower back, and shoulders during the swing can cause severe injuries and ruin a golfer's career. Fred Couples is an example of a player who is limited by physical injury. He has suffered from lower-back problems the last three years, which has caused him to miss several tournaments. If he plays every day he stays fit, but when he takes a layoff of a few days, problems start. Golfers who practice and play regularly should consult with a physical therapist as part of a total training regimen.

A physical therapist will do an extensive evaluation of your joint flexibility. He may also test your muscular strength and look for muscle symmetry. He can find any weak links in your overall fitness that impact your golf swing. A physical therapist understands the limitations of the body. He can work with your swing coach to help you develop a fluid and anatomically correct golf swing that allows for these limitations. He can also recommend specific stretching exercises to increase flexibility and reduce the risk of injury, and give you exercises to strengthen and tone the muscles used in the golf swing. Chapter Seven discusses common golf injuries, explains how to avoid injury, and offers specific exercises to reduce your risk of injury.

6. Eating to Score

A diet that provides proper nutrition should be a part of everyone's lifestyle, especially people who play a sport. During play, a golfer's blood sugar level can go down to hypoglycemic levels. Special chemicals in the brain needed for concentration and muscular coordination can become depleted during a long round of golf—say, a four-to-five hour round. Add the stress of competition, and a golfer's body can go into a depressed condition if it runs low on energy and minerals. If you golf, your body requires a constant supply of energy to perform at optimal levels.

Many people eat only what appeals to them and pay no attention to nutrition. Only when a life-threatening illness or other serious problem occurs, and the doctor says to eat better, do these people change their eating habits. Athletes today are more aware of the importance of diet in attaining peak performance. A good diet helps to improve endurance, power, and stamina by improving the oxygen-carrying catalysts in the blood, boosts your immune system and helps ward off disease and infection, and can help you live longer by reducing your risk of heart disease and other health problems, such as high blood pressure, diabetes, and arthritis. These conditions can be controlled and even corrected through diet.

Today we have diets that are specific to each sport—that is, they take into account the physical demands of the sport. Ideally, you should visit a qualified sports nutritionist. Every person has a different lifestyle, with changing eating patterns and different nutritional needs, and you want a diet that is specific for you. A sports nutritionist can perform an analysis of your current diet and recommend changes based on your individual needs. In Chapter Eight, I get you started on your way toward eating for better golfing.

7. COURSE MANAGEMENT PREPARATION

Another important part of your practice regimen is course management. This is simply the ability to study the course so you can score your best that day regardless of your ballstriking. Scoring is the name of the game in golf. When you write a number on the scorecard, no one knows how you made birdie, par, or bogey. The only thing that counts is finding the most efficient way to get the ball into the hole. It's not like diving or figure skating. You are not judged on technical merit or artistic value.

Course management has three parts: studying the course during a practice round, making a game plan or a strategy for playing the course, and carrying out your game plan. If you have local knowledge of the golf course, you can start the process of course management even before the practice round. If you can't play a practice round, however, the next best thing is to walk the course and take notes.

Why do tour pros play practice rounds? So they know when they should hit, say, a 3-wood on a tight hole. Or to calculate how many yards it is to carry a fairway bunker. Or to know how close the water hazard is from the back of the green. During a practice round, you should study the design of the course. The designer has put obstacles in your path. Your job is to find out how you should maneuver around those obstacles. You should take note of the slope of the greens, the direction of the grain on the greens, trouble in the landing areas, et cetera.

The practice round is a good time to decide what club to hit off each tee. It is also a good time to pick targets in the fairway and on the greens. You should note what side of the fairway to hit to for the best possible approach, and become familiar with the greens so you know what side of a particular green to hit your approach shots. Armed with this information, you can play smart golf by keeping the ball in play and playing to your strengths.

The second part of the course management process is developing a game plan that draws on your strengths and minimizes your weaknesses. Once you decide on a specific game plan, it's important to stick to your plan but be flexible when necessary. The goal of your plan should be to master the fundamentals of scoring, which include knowing when and where to lay up, getting up and down, making saving par putts, converting birdie putts, and, when you miss greens, leaving the ball in the best spot to get up and down. When Ben Crenshaw lays up on a par 5, he has an exact yardage in mind for his approach to the green. He has eliminated the decision of what club to hit. He knows that a full sand wedge goes 90 yards if it is struck solidly. Chapter Nine discusses how to score your best by developing a game plan and playing smart golf.

8. The Preround Prep

A training program would not be complete without some attention to a preround warm-up. If you neglect a preround warm-up, you will not be fully prepared to play your best. Getting off to a bad start in the round can give you a bad attitude for the entire round. The goal in a warm-up is different from that of a practice.

A warm-up has four purposes: to get loose, to focus the mind, to build up your confidence, and to gain a feel for your swing and tune up your touch on the greens. This is the time to get your "game face" on. At the same time, you should review your game plan, get focused for the opening holes, and hone your touch so you can play your best right out of the gate. In Chapter Ten, you'll learn the proper steps in a warm-up routine, tested by tour pros, so you will be ready to play your best. There I give you an example of a one-hour precompetition warm-up routine, covering everything you need to know to play great golf, from stretching to focusing your mind.

GETTING STARTED WITH YOUR PRACTICE PLAN

Your dream pushes you to achieve greatness. Your mission defines the path you will use to reach your dream. Your goals are the stepping-stones that give daily and weekly direction so you can achieve your mission. I always say that focusing on the process is what brings good results: striving for your goals is more important than getting there. Setting a schedule and weekly goals for practice and competition is an excellent way to keep you focused on the process. As you accomplish your daily and weekly goals, your confidence grows with each new achievement.

Goals should be specific, measurable, and attainable. They should address all areas of training—that is, you should have mental goals, physical goals, practice goals, and performance goals. Let's start by examining your practice priorities.

WHAT ARE YOUR PRACTICE PRIORITIES?

Ask yourself the following questions to prioritize your practice:

1. What areas of my game (putting, chipping, driving, etc.) need the most improvement?
2. What areas of my game have I neglected to practice in the past?
3. What type of training do I need to spend more time on?
4. What areas of training have I neglected to work on?
5. Do I need to find and meet with a swing coach, physical therapist, sports psychologist, or nutritionist?

THE OBJECTIVES OF A PRACTICE PLAN

It is vitally important to lay out your objectives for a practice plan. A plan contains the goals you want to accomplish—and the activities that will bring about those goals. Your plan should include goals that address the eight areas of your mission, discussed previously.

1. Make a list of your "training areas," from most needed to least needed, based on your current program. Include all the areas discussed in this chapter.
2. Assess your available time and decide how often you will get instruction and practice.
3. Decide what mental skills you need to improve and how often you will work on those.
4. Determine if you need to make changes in your diet and how often you will exercise each week.
5. Set specific, measurable goals for each skill you want to improve, such as exercising three times per week for one hour.
6. Revise your plan as often as needed.

Here are some tips for setting goals for your plan: Set difficult but attainable goals based on your present skill level, which can be measured by your statistical performance in various skill tests or on-course performance. Each goal should have a time frame (one hour, one week, one month, etc.) for its attainment. Evaluate often how you are doing, and revise your goals as you achieve them. Strengthen your commitment to improvement by rewarding yourself for achieving a goal—buy yourself a gift, for example.

FINAL THOUGHTS

The following list summarizes the areas of a total practice plan. You should assess your current situation in each of these areas to determine the strengths and weaknesses in your game. With this information, you can then prioritize a training regimen. Set specific goals for each of the training areas:

- Quality instruction: Find a qualified instructor who can teach in your "language."
- Focused practice: Use quality and focused practice to improve faster with less time wasted.
- Mental-game training: Find or call a sports psychologist who specializes in working with golfers.
- Getting fit: Set aside time in your schedule to exercise at least three times a week for one hour a day.
- Avoiding injury: Understand the biomechanics of the body and apply this information to your golf swing. Develop a more efficient swing with less wear and tear on the body.
- Proper nutrition and diet: Pay attention to diet and nutrition that improve overall health. Proper diet also leads to better energy, less fatigue, and better concentration during play.
- Course management: Studying the course and making a game plan for each tournament round helps you play smart golf.
- Proper warm-up: A good warm-up routine helps you be loose, confident, and focused for the first tee shot and beyond.

CHAPTER THREE

GETTING THE MOST OUT OF YOUR GOLF LESSONS

Finding the best instructor for your game is not an easy task. You know already if you have taken lessons from different golf instructors that no two are alike. Golf instructors have different backgrounds and teaching philosophies. They use distinct communication techniques and training methods to help you learn a golf swing. You'll find that some instructors can help you improve better than others because their teaching style is better suited to your personality, ability level, and the way you learn. That's why you need to do your homework when looking for an instructor. And if you already work with an instructor, you'll want to do all you can to get the most out of your lessons and practice time. This chapter will help you do just that.

Many of the best players in the world are not self-taught. Ernie Els, Tiger Woods, and Greg Norman continually hone their games with the help of instructors. With the teaching aids available today, you can learn a golf swing without personal instruction, but you will improve faster—with more permanent changes—by working with a trained teaching professional. The purpose of this chapter is to help you find the best golf instructor for you and to show you how to maximize each and every lesson you take.

THE GOALS OF EFFECTIVE LESSONS

Just as no two golf teachers teach the same, not all golf lessons are the same. The ultimate purpose of a golf lesson is to improve the efficiency and consistency of a player's swing so he can play better on the course. The instructor identifies problem areas, develops a strategy for change, then gives specific instruction to the student about how to improve the swing. An important part of taking golf instruction is to learn drills and mental images that bring about changes more efficiently. The student must then practice the changes, but this must be effective practice. Effective practice means using sources of feedback (training aids, video, a teacher, etc.) that ensure that the student is working on the proper swing. The cycle is repeated when the instructor evaluates the student's progress and determines if he is practicing correctly—that is, if the correct swing changes are being made.

Understanding the learning process can make you a better student, which will help you improve your golf swing faster. First, a golf teacher will use a trained eye for evaluating your swing and will provide direction for improvement based on your goals and the amount of time you can practice and play. Instructors realize that not everyone has aspirations of playing professional golf or can practice five hours a day, every day.

The last 25 years have seen remarkable equipment and ball improvements, but average handicaps have not improved. How fast you improve your swing depends mostly on your commitment to practice. How much and how fast you improve also depend on other factors, including skill level, physical ability, practice time, and productiveness of practice. You can't change the abilities you are born with, but you can control your quality of practice. And keep in mind that how much you improve will depend to a great extent on your current skill level. A 2-handicap player, for example, has less room for improvement than a 15-handicap player. But whatever your skill level, practice, repetition, and correct feedback are all needed for learning and positive change to occur. Don't expect to play better without practicing what you learn and applying it to your game.

As I mentioned earlier, the instruction you receive must be consistent with your abilities, body type, and size. Don't forget that you are trying to develop a golf swing that is right for you. Not everyone can swing like Steve Elkington, and pretty golf swings don't win tournaments. If this were true, then those players would win everything, and that's not the case. Jim Furyk is a good example of a player who has a swing that some people think is not sound, yet is repeatable and functional. Furyk knows his swing and has developed the proper compensations to make it work and make it repeatable. He knows that his swing produces a certain shot pattern that breeds consistency and confidence. That's exactly the goal—to develop confidence and consistency in a swing that is right for you.

THE ILLUSION OF FEEL

Have you ever seen your golf swing on video and said, "My swing feels so much different than it looks"? How your swing feels paints a picture in your mind of what it looks like from an observer's view, but that picture seldom matches what an observer's view or what your swing looks like on videotape. You might feel you are swinging well, but the videotape indicates otherwise. That's why working with a trained instructor is so important to improving your game. Your sense of feel—your sensory feedback—may be very fine-tuned but fails to tell you what's really happening. For example, even a slight alteration in your swing may sometimes feel more like a tremendous change than is actually apparent.

PGA teaching professional Mike Bender tells a story that illustrates this point. Mike once said to one student he was working with, "I'm going to videotape your swing now." The student, whom we'll call Paul, said, "Which swing do you want to see?" Mike asked, "How many swings do you have?" Paul said, "I have at least five different swings!" Mike asked Paul to show him three of his five swings. After videotaping Paul's swings, the two went off to review the video. On the way, Mike asked Paul what he felt the differences were in his swings. Paul replied, "The first one is my Jack Nicklaus swing, where I swing the club very upright. The second one is my baseball swing, where I swing the club very flat and around my body. The third is my compact swing, where I keep my right elbow close to my side." While reviewing the video, Paul was shocked to find that all three swings looked identical. This story exemplifies the main reason why changing the golf swing is difficult, and why to practice effectively you must have appropriate feedback (video, training aids, instructor, etc.). Later, we discuss different types of feedback you can use to improve the quality of your practice (also refer to Chapter Four).

FINDING A QUALIFIED INSTRUCTOR

What's the best way to go about finding a golf instructor? As with any other professional, you should research a teacher's qualifications and reputation in your local area. PGA professionals who specialize in teaching are the best place to start. Many club members feel obligated to take lessons from their local club professional, but if you are serious about improving your game, he may not be the best choice. Teaching professionals who specialize in instruction are usually more qualified than club professionals who teach part-time. If you had a heart condition, you wouldn't see a general practitioner; you would see a specialist, a cardiologist. Golf instructors should be selected in the same way.

You can use any of several references to find an instructor with a good reputation. One is the PGA office in your area. Call your local club or range and ask for the number of the nearest PGA section or chapter (in many cases, the PGA of America has several chapters in each section). The section or chapter office personnel will be glad to tell you the names of outstanding instructors in the area—perhaps some who have won awards for their efforts. Another source is *GOLF Magazine*'s list of the top 100 teaching professionals in the country. Or check with good players in your area.

Next, ask each prospective instructor for a list of students he teaches. These students will have firsthand knowledge of what the instructor teaches. Contact these students and ask about their experience with the instructor. Ask them if their game has improved while working with the teacher. Ask what the teacher focuses on in the lessons. Does he cover all phases of the game or just the full swing?

Interview each prospective teacher and ask about his teaching philosophy and style. A teacher should be able to answer the question Why do you teach the way you teach? and have a sound philosophy backed by solid experience and proven results with other players. The instructor's answer should make good sense to you. Does he have experience in a variety of teaching environments and situations? You want an instructor who has experience working with players of all levels. As an example of an instructor's philosophy, let's look at Mike Bender's:

My philosophy of the golf swing is to work in a direction that is going to make each student's swing more efficient. To do that, you need to eliminate excess moving parts. This means swinging the hands, arms, and club around a fixed axis on a plane throughout the entire swing, where the club shaft, arms, and clubhead are on plane throughout the swing. Perfecting these movements will lead to a very efficient swing that will hold up under pressure and last a lifetime.

Make sure to ask the instructor about his playing experience. You want a teaching pro who specializes in instruction, but one who plays well is a bonus.

The ideal golf instructor also has a background in or knowledge of kinesiology, motor behavior, and biomechanics. Better instructors understand how the body works and its limitations. Mike Bender, for example, has worked closely with a physical therapist and exercise physiologist, who has given him an understanding of the human body, the body's limitations, and how differences in body types affect the golf swing. This is important, because you don't want an instructor who teaches every student the same golf swing. Some students are limited in how they can swing because of joint structure, past injuries, or body type. As a student, you want to feel comfortable that your instructor is capable of teaching a swing that is right for you.

What are the personal characteristics you should look for in an instructor? First, an instructor should be willing to listen to you, have an open mind, and be patient with your needs. Second, it's important to find an accessible instructor. If you commit to a long-term program, you need someone who has time to work with you on a regular basis. Third, this person should show a genuine interest in your game and progress and not be in it just for the money. Find out if you can ask questions over the phone when you need help.

Here is a list of a few questions you might ask a potential instructor:

1. How accessible are you?
2. How far in advance do I need to call for a lesson?
3. What do you recommend with respect to frequency of lessons?
4. Do you have a package rate for a series of lessons?
5. Do you have any references I can call?
6. What is your philosophy of the golf swing?
7. How do you run your lessons? What is the format?
8. What areas of the game do you teach? Do you specialize in any particular areas?
9. Do you use training aids or video?
10. May I call you between lessons with questions about my game? Do you charge for this?
11. How do you help me take my game from the practice tee to the golf course?
12. Do you teach course management or offer playing lessons?

WHAT SHOULD YOU EXPECT?

When it comes to golf instruction, everybody has different expectations. Some are perfectly legitimate: you should expect to receive the undivided attention of the instructor, for example. Nothing is more unnerving than working with a teacher who is distracted during the lesson. Good teachers use video, audio, training aids, feedback, and practice drills to enhance retention and to quicken learning.

Other expectations may be arbitrary or unreasonable. What are your expectations for improvements in your game? Most golfers we know have very high expectations, but it's hard to determine how much improvement you can reasonably expect. Many variables are at work here. Your present skill level, amount and quality of practice, physical ability, previous knowledge of the swing, and level of commitment to improvement are just a few of the things that influence how much and how fast you will learn.

One key factor you *can* control is commitment to getting better. As we've seen, even many of the best players in the world, such as Tiger Woods, have employed full-time instructors. Why does the best player in the world have a full-time instructor? The answer is that he is always trying to improve his game. Golf instruction involves a continual learning process and a commitment to getting better over time.

Golf is a game of a lifetime. Not because you can play it for your lifetime, but because it takes a lifetime to master.

—*Bill Strausbaugh, golf instructor*

WHAT IS YOUR DOMINANT LEARNING STYLE?

The best instructors mold their teaching style to the needs of the student. In other words, a good teacher knows how to teach to your learning style. What is a learning style? It's the way that you process information in your world. Your schoolteachers most likely used several ways to teach the same information—visual, auditory, kinesthetic, and experiential. That's because people learn via different perceptual styles and at various speeds. It's important to find an instructor who uses a style of teaching that suits your learning style, although most instructors know how to get their message across using several different styles.

How do you determine your dominant learning style? Close your eyes for a moment. . . . Experience yourself on the driving range at your home course. Put yourself in that experience. Take a few swings without a ball. Good. Now experience yourself hitting two or three shots. . . . OK. What did you choose to focus on? Were you more tuned in to the feel of the swing, such as your balance, or the feel of your muscles? Did you focus more on the visual experience of hitting balls—"seeing" the ball in the air and watching the club as you took it back? Or did you focus more on the sound of a solid shot? Maybe you had a combination of images, such as feeling the golf swing and seeing the shot. Whatever you chose to experience, most likely that is your dominant style of learning. Also, how do you normally prepare for a shot? Do you focus on the flight of the ball? Do you feel a good shot before you hit it? Or do you hear the swoosh of the club in the air and the sound of contact?

One learning style is auditory or verbal. If you are this type of learner, the instructor telling you how to swing the club may work best for you. If you are a visual learner, you learn faster with pictures or by having the instructor demonstrate the golf swing. If you are a kinesthetic, or feel, learner, you would be better matched with an instructor who uses metaphors and images of how the swing should feel. For example, your instructor may teach the downswing by having you imagine skipping a stone over water with your right hand and arm. This action mimics the proper position of the arm while performing the downswing. Or he might put you in the proper position or use drills and training aids to create the proper feel.

Not all golf instructors are aware of different learning styles. An instructor may be comfortable with using only one teaching style, such as visual. This may be very effective for a visual player, but it may not be the best style for you. Find a teacher who has an instruction style that matches your learning style as closely as possible. As we saw earlier, most good teachers know how to get their message across in several ways.

PRACTICE, FEEDBACK, AND REPETITION

The standard teaching model today follows this sequence: the student gets a lesson from his instructor; the instructor gives the student information and techniques to improve his game; and the student practices what was taught on his own. What's the problem with this model? The student is left to practice what the instructor said without supervision.

An instructor must do more than just teach you about how to swing. He must show you how to practice it correctly (see Chapter Four). He should also show you practice drills so that you know you are practicing what you were taught. A good instructor will have several methods that show you if you are practicing the proper way, such as video, training aids, practice stations, and specific drills.

Assuming that you already have an instructor and are getting quality instruction, what else can you do to make your effort pay off? Whether it's a physical or mental lesson, many players have a misconception that an instructor can "fix" them in one or two lessons. But it's not that easy. You can't buy a good golf swing or mental game. Experts say that it takes 60 days of practice and several repetitions a day to develop a new habit, provided you are practicing correctly with each swing. Motor patterns do not change overnight. We do know that the more efficient your practice is, the faster you will ingrain a new habit.

Practice doesn't make perfect, it makes permanent.
Perfect practice makes perfect.

—Mike Bender, PGA teaching professional

I worked with a player named Ralph who was frustrated with the lack of progress in his game. Even after many lessons with several renowned instructors, he hadn't shown improvement and thought anxiety and tension were the root of his problem. I asked Ralph how much time he practiced what he learned in the lessons. Ralph said, "I don't have time to practice—maybe one hour a week." Ralph assumed that he could just show up and pay for a lesson and his game would improve overnight.

Improvement occurs only when practice and repetition are part of the learning process. A lesson only initiates the learning cycle; it leads to understanding of the golf swing. Without practice, repetition, feedback, and fine tuning, no real improvement can take place.

As we've seen, an instructor first identifies problem areas and weaknesses in the swing and develops a strategy for change. The swing or putting stroke is evaluated and changes to be made are identified. Drills, training aids, mental images, or metaphors are used in the lesson to help the student understand the changes and practice them efficiently. At this point, no permanent changes have occurred yet. Only after practice and more practice—the right kind of practice—does real learning occur. If you practice the wrong way, you only get good at doing the wrong things. As you practice, your own sensory feedback and external sources of information are necessary to tell you if you are on track. The final step is to have a trained eye reevaluate your swing and see if you are making progress.

Whether you are addressing a physical or mental aspect of your game, learning occurs over weeks and months, and only if you practice what you were taught. So the real work starts after the lesson, and even then your swing does not change overnight. Too many players expect a magical quick-fix. The reality is that change comes between lessons while you are executing your practice plan.

A favorite quote of Mike Bender, which he saw posted in a pro shop, stated:

> *One lesson, $1,000. Five lessons, $150.*
> *If you want a miracle, you have to pay for it.*
>
> *—Pro shop owner*

Should you work with more than one instructor at a time? In most cases, this is not a good idea. I have worked with several players who jumped from teacher to teacher, searching in vain for "the secret." Generally speaking, you should avoid changing golf instructors from one lesson to the next. However, this may be a good idea if you need to consult a specialist in one area of your game—your short game, long game, mental game, or strategy, for example.

A good golf instructor knows that the game involves more than just hitting full shots, and he will include lessons in all parts of the game, not just the full swing. You should be receiving instruction on chipping, pitching, putting, sand shots, and specialty shots. An instructor should be able to teach at least the basics of course management, the mental game, and preshot routines. Lessons should not be confined to the practice range. Ask your teacher to play a round or two with you while you work on course management skills.

RECORDING THE LESSON AND USING FEEDBACK TO ENHANCE LEARNING

You won't remember everything you were taught in a lesson. So, to get the most out of each lesson, you should make a record of what you worked on. You can use videotape, audiotape, a written summary of the lesson, or a combination of all three. Mike Bender, for example, videotapes each lesson, summarizes the drills for the student on the video, and gives the tape to the student. The student brings the tape back for each lesson to add new material and keep track of progress.

If your teacher doesn't provide a visual, auditory, or written record of each lesson, ask if you yourself can record the lesson. You can come to practice with an audio or video recorder. Or you may want to use a notebook to take notes during and after the lesson. Or use a dictation unit to remind you of what to work on in practice, what drills to practice, and what to discuss with your instructor. Mike Bender and I recommend that you keep a notebook or folder in which to put notes and handouts, and to write questions to ask your instructor during the next lesson.

Feedback lets a student know for sure if he is practicing correctly. Your instructor is one source of feedback, but he can't be by your side during every swing. It's up to you (with guidance from your instructor) to monitor your swing when you practice on your own. To learn, you need both internal and external forms of feedback. We have discussed how internal feedback (the feel of the swing) can be misleading. That is why external feedback (what is called "external knowledge about performance") is so important. Seeing yourself on video and swinging in front of a mirror are examples of external forms of feedback.

Again, golfers have their own internal mechanisms of feedback, such as the feel of the movement, sense of balance, and information about the flight or trajectory of the shot. However, the ball's flight does not always tell you if you are swinging correctly. Sometimes a bad swing produces a good shot, or a good swing produces a bad shot, especially if you are in the middle of altering your swing. Players who are changing their swings may make a good swing at the ball and perform the move 95 percent correctly—but still hit a bad shot. The clubface may be open at impact, say, and the ball may start right of the target line.

Why are training aids so important? As discussed earlier, the feel of your swing can be deceptive. What you feel via your senses does not always tell you what you're actually doing. Videotape or drills that employ training aids give you direct feedback about your swing. This can be enormously helpful and accelerate your learning, especially when you practice alone. With a training aid, you are not relying on feel alone. The aid gives you objective, accurate feedback or knowledge about the appropriateness of each swing by telling you when you did or did not make the proper swing.

A training aid is less effective when it does all the work for you. What's an example of a good training aid—one that gives the student feedback but does not do all the work for the student? Let's say Mike is working with a student who loses knee flex during the backswing. First he teaches the correct knee flex. Then he places a plastic rod against the student's right knee and tells him to make a few swings. The student can immediately feel when he doesn't maintain knee flex

FIGURE 3.1

A training aid should give feedback about body position during the swing, but not do the work for the student. This speeds learning and enhances retention.

in his right leg throughout the swing. The training aid teaches a key movement in the swing but does not do the work for the student (by forcing the proper amount of knee flex during the swing), thus helping the student learn the feel of a correct swing faster because he creates the proper movement.

Your instructor can also help you set up a practice plan and schedule. The weaker parts of your game, identified by your teacher, should be a practice priority. Your teacher can help you decide how often and how long you should practice each area of your game. Then it's important to know the best way to practice to get the most out of each lesson and your practice time (this is the topic of Chapter Four).

Also develop a lesson schedule with assistance of your instructor. Initially, the instruction may be as frequent as once a week. Later, you might meet once a month to assess your progress. Identify some goals—what changes you will make—then decide on a weekly practice schedule, what skills and drills you will work on, and how much time you will devote to each area. Your plan should include all facets of the game, including the full swing, putting, chipping, wedge play, and bunker work. Too many players neglect the most important parts of the game—putting and chipping. If you are not hitting enough greens, a good short game will help you score your best.

FINAL THOUGHTS

In this chapter you have learned that you need to play an active role in your golf lessons. The following list summarizes how you can get the most out of your instruction:

- Find an instructor who can teach in the language that you learn best (visual, auditory, kinesthetic).
- To find the best instructor, do your homework and ask questions, check references, and interview candidates.
- Once instruction has begun, it's up to you to put your lessons to work with quality practice, feedback, and repetition.
- You won't remember everything you learn in a lesson. That's why you should videotape it or take notes during and after the lesson.
- Ask for drills or training aids that will tell you when you are performing the desired move, thus speeding your learning.
- Ask your instructor to help you develop a practice schedule, and find out how long you will need to make suggested changes.

CHAPTER FOUR

DEVELOPING SOUND PRACTICE HABITS

Whether you play golf for recreation or competitively, focused, quality practice will help you improve faster. How can you be more effective at practice without spending more time? The answer is by integrating proven methods of motor learning and sports psychology into your practice to speed learning and retention. The best players in the world know how to practice effectively so they can play their best on the course. If you want to make better use of your practice time, or if you hit the ball great on the range but can't take your "practice game" to the course, you will be especially interested in this chapter.

The typical golfer—let's call him John—takes two favorite clubs to the driving range, a 7-iron and driver. He starts by smashing balls with his driver one after the other down the range. John doesn't bother to pick out targets, because his goal is to hit balls over the fence at the end of the range. After raking in ball after ball and hitting a few drivers, he grabs the 7-iron. He hits to the same 150-yard flag without varying the shape of his shots, changing clubs, or picking a new target. He hits and rakes with no rest and no thought between shots, mindlessly beating the balls. This is great exercise, but poor practice.

This example, although extreme, shows how a great many golfers practice today. John is not engaging in focused, goal-oriented practice. In other sports, athletes practice and play on the same field of play. Tennis players practice and play on a tennis court. Basketball players practice and play on a basketball court. Baseball players practice and play on a baseball field. But golfers practice on a range and play on a course—two different experiences. Golfers are forced to practice under conditions that don't match the golf course, which makes the quality of their practice even more important. Quality practice means a goal-focused and concentrated attitude, something to which most players are not accustomed. Quality practice involves concentration, creativity, imagination, and the propensity to practice in the same manner in which you play on the course.

Quality practice is focused, goal-oriented practice. If you practice the wrong way, you just get good at the wrong thing.

Sometimes we see players who look like scratch golfers on the range, but when they play competitively they are a 15-handicap. That's because every shot hit on the golf course is unique, with its own challenge. Playing on a course requires a higher level of thought and imagination. You are forced to think about the lie of the ball, distance to the target, wind direction and intensity, conditions of the course, and other factors that influence club selection and shot-making. Other, unobservable factors increase the challenge of each shot even more: the thoughts, images, level of focus, and confidence you have during each shot. Thus, range practice often doesn't translate well to playing on the course.

In addition, you never have the same putt twice during a round of golf. The length, the speed, the amount of break, and the look of the shot change with every putt. Practice greens simply do not present the same challenges you get on the course. Hence, your putting practice should involve learning to read greens, to develop imagination and visual skills, and to improve touch. Good putting practice is not about grooving a perfect putting stroke or hitting a hundred 10-foot putts.

Like John, most players don't know what and how to practice. After a lesson with an instructor, most golfers are left to fend for themselves on the practice tee. This is why it's very important to get your instructor involved in your practice (see Chapter Three).

Another good way to practice is to simulate on-course situations. Peter Vidmar, an Olympic gymnast, trained this way for competition before the 1984 Olympics. Peter's goal was to make his practice as close to a real meet as possible, with the same distractions and emotions that go with competition. At the UCLA gymnasium, Peter and his teammates wore competition uniforms, played crowd noise, and introduced other distractions present during a meet. At the start of each routine, Peter raised his hand to his coach (just as he must do in a meet for the judges) to signal he was ready for the routine. In his mind, he was competing.

This type of practice—what's called specificity training—increased Peter's focus and intensity, which helped him compete at a higher level. During competition, he simply imagined he was back at the gym going through his normal practice routine.

Many athletes, including some of the world's great golfers, use specificity training like this when they practice. They practice with the same intensity of mind they have while playing a round. In fact, many new practice facilities have been built to resemble small golf courses so golfers can practice in a setting that approximates what they will see during competitive play. The goal of this chapter is to teach you how to practice effectively and to give you specific drills that you can modify and apply to your game.

KEYS TO EFFECTIVE PRACTICE

Quality practice is based on four general guidelines. It should be goal-driven, focused, varied, and applied to what you do on the course. What you practice should be specific, and it should be determined by a goal you want to reach. You should strive to have the same intensity and focus in practice that you maintain on the course. It's important to diversify your practice—that is, practice both putting and driving—and to vary each shot you hit. Finally, it's best to engage in specificity practice so your practice transfers well to the golf course. If you apply these guidelines, you'll be engaging in quality practice.

There are two distinct forms of practice. One is mechanics practice, in which you attempt to master the fundamentals of putting, chipping, pitching, and full shots. Here you become competent with the precise movements of the golf swing. The second type of practice is shotmaking, which integrates the mental skills and course strategies that are critical for playing the scoring shots once you have learned an effective golf swing. Here imagination, confidence, preshot routine, and touch and feel are developed, refined, and integrated with your skills and knowledge about course management (see Chapter Nine) to produce your best shot.

ONE STEP AT A TIME

The human mind processes information in a serial fashion, one thought or image after another. Your mind can focus on only one thought or idea at a time. It cannot process making changes in grip, posture, setup, and backswing all at the same time. In other words, you can overload yourself with too much information. The key is to simplify your thought process and practice one skill or mechanical change at a time.

If an instructor makes four swing changes, for example, pick one change to work on at a time. Likewise, stick to one swing thought or one drill at a time. When you are comfortable with that change, move to the next one. Later, you can put the pieces together into a complete whole, which is vital for transferring what you have learned to the golf course.

NO OVERNIGHT FIXES

I'm often asked how long it takes to make a swing change. The answer depends on the person and how much time he devotes to practice. Some experts say it takes several repetitions a day for as many as 60 days to form a habit. Most instructors agree that it takes at least 21 days to create a habit. Others suggest that it takes three-thousand repetitions to form a habit. I know some instructors who tell their students that they are on a four-year plan. That may seem like a lot of time to remake a swing, but it may be necessary if you don't have the time to practice every day. You can't expect to make significant changes overnight—or in a week, for that matter. When you make a swing change, you have to extinguish a bad habit and replace it with a new habit. This is harder to do than learning something in which you have not formed any bad habits. That's why children are such good learners: they haven't had enough time to learn bad habits.

USE FEEDBACK TO ENHANCE LEARNING

Why do most students hit the ball better when taking a lesson from an instructor? The reason is that an instructor can give you immediate input about your swing. This input tells you that you are (or are not) performing the swing correctly, which is critical for learning. When you are alone hitting balls, you don't have this feedback. Instead, you must rely on the feel of your swing and the result of the shot, which can be deceptive.

You learn much faster if you use external sources of feedback (or knowledge about your performance). A good source of external feedback is a video camera. Videotape doesn't lie. Your goal is to equate the feel of the golf swing (what you think you are doing) with how you are actually swinging.

If you don't have access to a video camera, you can use training aids that give you immediate and accurate information about each swing you take. For example, Mike Bender uses a simple drill to help correct swing path. It requires only two tees. Mike says this drill is helpful for students who come over the top and slice the ball. He puts a ball on one tee and places another tee in the ground four inches away from the ball and just to the right of the target line. His students have to hit both tees on the downswing, which promotes an inside-to-outside swing. The player gets instant feedback when he hits or doesn't hit the tees.

A good instructor will suggest training aids or provide drills that tell you if you are practicing correctly. Many training aids can be used both at the practice range and at your home or hotel, depending on your schedule and the weather conditions.

PLAY GOLF SHOTS—DON'T BEAT BALLS

The most important type of practice is playing actual golf shots. Professional golfers would never just beat balls or hit putts without a purpose and complete focus, but that's how most amateurs practice.

How do you play a shot on the course? You pick a target, determine the distance, and select a club. Then you imagine and/or feel the shot and do your normal preshot routine. Your focus and intensity on the course is heightened because of the mental processes needed to prepare for a shot. Your practice should mimic this process. You should play shots with focus and intention, not just smash balls one after the next. Pick a target each time you hit a shot. Imagine the ball flying to the target. Practice going through your normal aim, alignment, and setup procedure. This is how you should play shots on the course, so why not do it in practice?

The golf shot should begin well before you start the club back—with a decision, a plan, and a rehearsal of the shot. If you want to avoid mindlessly raking and hitting balls, a routine can help. It's not necessary or practical to hit every shot with your preshot routine; instead, shoot for hitting half of your practice balls using your routine. The best way to develop a good preshot routine is to practice it on the range. Developing your routine on the course is not the answer. It should feel natural and instinctive. Prepare for a shot in practice the same way you hit shots on the course.

Your routine for both full shots and putting should include five parts: specific plan, positive image, active rehearsal, target or feel focus, and execution. In the planning stage, you are picking out a target and selecting the type of shot you want to hit. The next step is to visualize or feel the shot, thereby programming your body for execution. Then you rehearse the motion required for the shot with a practice swing. The last step is to focus your mind on a swing cue, image of the target, or the feel of a good shot, depending on your learning style and personal preference. I discuss how to develop a preshot routine in more detail in Chapter Five.

VARIETY IS THE SPICE OF GOLF

You use all your clubs when you play, so why not practice with everything in the bag? You might have a club or two you prefer, but how well can you hit a nonfavorite club when you have to on the course? If you are working on swing mechanics, by all means use your favorite club. But if you are practicing shotmaking, switch clubs often, and mix it up. Don't hit more than 10 shots in a row with the same club.

The best practice mimics the shots you anticipate playing in your next round. Many tour pros prepare for tournaments by hitting the exact shots they will need to hit on a particular course. For example, if you normally hit a driver and then a 7-iron on the first hole, hit these clubs in practice. If the next hole calls for a 2-iron off the tee, hit a 2-iron in practice. Practice all the clubs you expect to use on the course.

A main principle of motor learning is to practice in a variety of settings and conditions. In tennis, players are forced to play an infinite variety of shots. A player must hit a return shot with the ball bouncing in any direction or at any height—low, high, behind, curving—and when the player is running and off balance. In golf, you don't hit shots while you are running and the ball is not moving, but you must hit shots with different lies, distances, and weather conditions. This is part of what makes golf so interesting: you never have the same shot twice on the course. You are forced to hit uphill, downhill, sidehill, and flat-lie shots.

Be creative with practice so you will be confident with any shot you encounter during play. When Seve Ballesteros was a kid, he took only three or four clubs to play a course. He was forced to create shots that he wouldn't normally hit if he had a full set of clubs. He attributes his keen imagination on the golf course to these experiences.

You can vary practice in many ways. Besides switching clubs often on the range, you can vary the lie of the ball. Practice shots from perfect lies, buried lies, perched lies, divots, and sandy lies. Vary the trajectory and curve of the shot. Hit high and low shots, right-to-left and left-to-right shots, specialty shots, and half and full shots. You can change targets on each shot. Vary the terrain where you hit shots. Hit shots from uphill, downhill, and sidehill lies. You get the picture. Don't just hit balls from a flat, perfect lie to the same target. You hit all kinds of shots on the course, so why not get good at them in practice first?

INVOLVE YOUR CREATIVE MIND

Creativity is important to playing good golf, especially in the short game. Phil Mickelson has great imagination. He imagines and practices every possible situation he may encounter on the course. If he has to play a lob shot over a bunker and stop the ball fast, he knows how to hit the shot with confidence because he has practiced it. You may have to invent a shot on the course that you don't normally practice. Do you ever practice hitting shots around or under trees? Do you practice hitting shots out of divots? Do you practice full shots out of the bunker?

Practice specialty shots on the range that you might confront on the course, not just the shots you like to hit. Imagine you have to hit a low knock-down shot under a tree. Pretend you have to hit a high wedge over a tall tree in front of you. Imagine working the ball around a tree and hit a cut or a hook. In addition to practicing these shots, invent shots that you think you would never need to play on the course. This can only help your confidence when you find yourself in trouble and need to conceive a creative shot.

CHALLENGE YOURSELF

Many players find it hard to get excited about practice, which may cause their focus to be less than optimal. Granted, hitting shots on the range is not as thrilling as playing a shot on the 18th hole at

---

PATRICK'S PRACTICE PRINCIPLES FOR FULL GAME

1. *Focus on one goal at a time. Limit your focus to one move or change at a time.*

2. *Use some form of feedback when you practice so you know you are making the proper swing or doing the drill correctly.*

3. *Play golf shots; don't just hit balls on the range. Match your practice to how you play on the course.*

4. *Mix it up on the range; don't just hit to the same target with the same club every time.*

5. *Be creative with your practice and force yourself to practice specialty shots and off-the-wall shots.*

6. *Challenge yourself with goals and games to keep you interested, focused, and motivated.*

Pebble Beach. This is why some players hit the ball poorly on the range and 10 minutes later hit the ball well on the course.

For the golfer who lacks motivation to practice, hitting balls on the range can be very boring. This is why having a purpose, goals, stimulation, and challenges are so important in practice. Just as in Peter Vidmar's gymnastics example, you too can increase your intensity in practice. One way is to play competitive games on the range that stimulate and challenge you, such as "call your shot." In this game, you try to invent an impossible shot around the green, and you and a partner have to hit the same shot. You take turns calling the shot. Take it a step further and imagine that every putt you hit on the practice green is to win the U.S. Open. Although it's still practice, this approach will help you come close to matching the emotions and intensity you need on the course.

Challenge yourself to reach a specific goal. Pick out flags, bunkers, or trees that designate boundaries of the fairway. Set a goal to hit, say, 10 out of 14 fairways in an imaginary fairway in the

FIGURE 4.1

Practice uncommon shots, such as shots from under a tree, so you will be prepared to hit any shot on the course.

range. You can increase the challenge by hitting different types of shots. Start the ball down the left side of the fairway and have it finish in the center, and vice versa.

GOLF COURSE PRACTICE

If the best way to practice is to practice how you play, then the best practice is on the golf course. This is why pros play practice rounds before a tournament. The conditions more closely match what's encountered in competition. Targets become more defined, every shot is different, and you have to switch clubs often. When the course is not crowded, you can hit three balls off the tee and play your worst ball. This will sharpen your short game on par 3s and make approach shots more difficult on longer holes. Experiment with using different clubs off the tees on the par-4 and -5 holes. This will give you the opportunity to hit different clubs into the green and be creative with your shotmaking.

KEYS TO IMPROVING SHORT-GAME PRACTICE

Golfers tend to neglect the short game. Most, given the choice, prefer to practice the long game, perhaps because of the glamor of hitting an accurate long drive. Fans love to watch John Daly or Tiger Woods hit a 300-yard tee shot. But the fact is that putting, chipping, and pitching account for more than 60 percent of the total number of shots you hit in a given round. I stress short-game practice because a player can shoot lower scores faster with small improvements in the short game. If you hit a bad drive or approach shot, all it takes is one good chip or putt to save par.

Putting accounts for around 40 percent of the game, but do you spend 40 percent of your practice time putting? Take a look at your putting statistics. If you have over 32 putts per round, your putting can improve. And if you are three-putting two times a round, that's two three-putts too many. How much time should you spend practicing your short game? A good rule is to spend at least half of your practice time on your short game. You take pressure off your long game when you are chipping and putting well. Hitting nine greens in regulation and shooting 72 is very satisfying and can build your confidence in your short game.

PUTTING PRACTICE

Great putting, as I describe in *The Mental Art of Putting,* is about developing a consistent stroke, gaining confidence, and forming good touch and visualization skills. As with the full swing, how and what you practice dictates how fast you will learn and improve. Research in motor learning suggests that practice is more effective when one's mind-set during practice matches the mind-set one maintains in competition. The purpose of putting practice is to groove a consistent and repeatable stroke; develop touch and control distance; enhance green reading and visualization skills; and improve putting confidence. Let's talk briefly about how to achieve each of these aims.

Grooving a Consistent and Repeatable Stroke

A good stroke is important to good putting, but you don't want to become preoccupied with developing a perfect stroke. More important is that you roll the ball on your intended line with the correct pace. Many different putting methods accomplish this. Spend 10 minutes a day checking the fundamentals of your stroke, but don't become obsessed with it; otherwise you won't putt your best. The more you change your putting method and search for the ideal stroke, the harder it is to develop a repeatable stroke that you have confidence in. Find one method and stick to it.

If you have one hour to practice, spend only 15 minutes working on stroke mechanics. Check your ball position, aim, alignment, and putter path, one at a time. Or devote 15 minutes to putting with a chalk line, putting board, or other training aid you prefer. A simple test of your stroke is to try to make 20 putts in a row from three feet. If you can do this, your stroke is good enough to make putts on a fairly consistent basis. Use most of your putting practice to develop touch, enhance visualization skills, and refine your preshot routine.

Developing Touch on the Greens

Great putting comes from having great touch. Watch any great putter, and you will see that he consistently controls the pace of his putts. Many great putters I work with believe that their putting success is attributable primarily to good touch. Why is touch so important? Touch is the ability to judge and control speed, and that's the key to making putts. Touch is necessary for two reasons: to hit longer putts close to the hole, and to select the right line given a certain pace on breaking putts. Picking the right line doesn't guarantee you will make the putt. On breaking putts, speed is just as important as line. You must judge the right speed given the line you selected. If hit too hard, a putt won't take the break; if hit too soft, a putt won't hold its line.

The key to developing touch is to practice *every* possible putt you may have on the course. If you practiced 10-footers all day, your

FIGURE 4.2

Lag to the fringe drill. This is an easy drill you can do on any green to help you develop touch and warm up for the round.

putting performance from 30 feet or longer would suffer. Practice from different lengths—10, 20, 30, 40, and 50 feet, and all distances in between. Vary your distances often. Breaking putts require both touch and imagination. Vary the type and severity of the putt's break. Hit left-to-right and right-to-left breaking putts. Hit putts with large breaks and small breaks. Hit double breakers. Vary the length of breaking putts. Hit putts uphill and downhill.

In the box on page 46, I describe five drills for developing touch. The key component of all the drills is for you to mix it up and vary your putting practice. Don't hit the same putt twice in a row. Also, putt with the balls you normally play because different balls feel and react differently.

Two skills are important in controlling distance. The first is judging how far to hit the putt, which comes from experience and your touch. The second is executing that feeling. Your goal then is to lock in the correct judgment (touch) and execute the needed effort control (feel) of each putt. When you practice these drills, don't think

PATRICK'S PRACTICE DRILLS TO IMPROVE TOUCH

1. *Four tees putting drill: Space four tees across the green at 20, 25, 30, and 35 feet. The goal is to hit a putt to the first tee but not more than two feet beyond. You start at the first tee, then move to the next tee. If you don't hit it to the tee or in the "good" zone, start over from the first tee. The drill is to hit eight consecutive putts (four up and four back). The key is to let your eyes guide your putter—don't try to hit the putt 20 feet, for example. To increase the difficulty of the drill, try it downhill.*

2. *Fine touch drill: Using several balls, hit your first putt about 6 feet. The goal of this drill is to hit each new putt just past the last putt and as close to it as possible. Hit your next putt just past that one, the next putt just past that one, and so on. Try to hit the balls as close together as possible up to 40 feet. The closer the balls are spaced, the better your touch.*

3. *Lag to the fringe drill: Starting in the center of the green, space 10 balls across a green about two feet part. Pick a spot on the collar of the green and hit each putt to that point. Focus on the speed of each putt as you take a practice stroke, and don't worry so much about direction. To enhance the drill, do it uphill and downhill. Hit as many different distances as possible—the longer the better.*

4. *Three cups drill: Using nine balls, find three cups on the green that line up in the same general direction. You should have one short, one medium, and one long putt. Hit one putt to each cup in random order. On each new putt, hit it to a different cup. Again, the goal is to focus on speed or pace.*

5. *Eyes closed drill: Using five balls, find a cup that is about 30 feet away. Hit each putt to the cup with your eyes closed. The goal is to judge if the putt was short, good, or long without looking. A good putt gets to the cup but no farther than two feet past the cup. When you correctly call out five putts in a row, change the distance of the putt. The longer the putt, the more difficult. This drill helps you to develop a feel for distance and how solidly you hit the putt.*

about the length of the stroke. Tune in to the feeling of your arms, the tempo of the putter, and the feeling of the putter impacting the ball. The ultimate goal is to look at a putt of any distance and instinctively react to the perceptual input from your eyes only, bypassing all conscious thought about how hard to hit the putt.

Improving Green Reading and Visualization Skills

I combine reading greens and visualization because they are closely linked. Reading greens is an art, but it's based on experience and ability to anticipate, or "see," the correct line. Several factors—such as the amount of slope, speed of the green, type of grass, and direction of the grain—influence what line you see in your mind. Fast greens break more given the same slope angle. Greens with more moisture do not break as much and are slower than a dry surface. The ball travels farther downgrain than if you putt against the grain. Often a strong-grained variety of grass such as Bermuda causes a putt to break differently, depending on if you are going downgrain or with the grain. Strong winds can also influence the roll of the ball, especially on fast greens. With experience your brain detects these influencing factors, and you become better at seeing the correct line. For a more in-depth discussion of reading greens, pick up a copy of *See It and Sink It* by Craig L. Farnsworth (1996). In the box on page 48, I give five drills to improve your visualization and green-reading skills.

Not every player can instinctively "see" a line. These players are simply not visual learners or performers. They rely on feel, and that's fine. For our purposes, I refer to visualization as the ability to use images, whether visual or feeling, to help you read greens. The putting drills described in the boxes on pages 46 and 48 are designed to heighten your sense of touch and green reading because they work jointly.

My favorite drill is the Three Bears Drill. The goal of this drill is to make breaking putts at various speeds. This drill forces you to see a different line each time and match it with the correct speed. Feedback is important here, as it is in any drill. Pay careful attention to how the ball breaks on various slopes, watch the ball as it turns, and imprint the image of the ball rolling into the hole. If you miss a putt, use the information to adjust your mental image and touch on the next putt.

PATRICK'S DRILLS FOR IMPROVING VISUALIZATION AND GREEN READING

1. *Three bears drill: This requires three balls and one cup on a sloped part of the green. Start with three 10-footers with right-to-left break. The goal is to hit three putts using three different lines: die it in, firm it in, and your own natural pace. Visualize three different lines and match the line with the pace of the putt. Focus on visualizing the line for each pace. See the ball enter the hole the last two feet. To vary this drill, hit putts from all sides of the hole (uphill, downhill, left to right, right to left) and from 10, 20, and 30 feet.*

2. *Visualizing a line with your eyes closed: Start with a straight 10-foot putt. Visualize a line on the green; then close your eyes and visualize the line. Stroke the putt with your eyes closed. Focus on seeing a line in your mind's eye and letting your body respond to that image. Progress to more difficult putts with more breaks and distance. Hit putts from all sides of the hole.*

3. *Reading putts with visualization: Start with a 20-foot putt breaking right to left. Standing behind the ball, visualize where the ball would finish if you putted it straight at the hole. If you see it finish three inches left of the hole, replay the putt in your mind and start it three inches right of the hole. Did you see it go into the hole? If yes, hit the putt with that line in mind. If not, replay the putt in your mind until you see it go into the hole. Make sure you see the ball travel along your line into the cup before you hit it. Repeat this process with 20 different putts with various breaks.*

4. *Reading putts as you approach the green: Set up a medium-length putt and walk off the green about 20 yards, keeping the ball between you and the hole. As you approach the green, notice the undulation to get a feel for how the putt breaks. Walk right into the address position without reading the putt further. Hit the putt with what you saw as you approached the green.*

5. *Reading the putt from the low side of the green: Your best read is from the low side of the green. On a sloping green, place a ball 20 feet above the hole. First, walk below the hole to the lowest side of the green and read the putt. Next, go to the high side of the green above the ball and reconfirm what you saw below the hole. If you see a different line above the hole, go back to the low side of the green and look again. Stick to what you saw on the low side of the green and play your putt. Hit 20 putts from above and below the hole, reading it from the low side of the green.*

Improve Putting Confidence

Confidence is the number-one ingredient of all of those that help you make putts on the course. You simply can't putt your best without confidence. Confidence develops first from holing putts in practice, then transferring that confidence to the course. Confidence starts on the practice green by developing *competence* in the specific skills required for good putting. These specific skills include the ability to read greens, aim, set up, hit the ball solidly, launch the ball on line, and control your pace. Improving touch and feel, improving visualization skills, and developing a focused putting routine are the mental abilities that develop putting confidence.

Besides these important skills, confidence comes from holing putts. That's why it's very important to see, feel, and hear the ball go into the hole. With each holed putt, you log the memory and image of the ball going into the hole. This means that, when you practice putting, you should hit several putts from a comfortable distance—

PATRICK'S PRACTICE DRILLS FOR DEVELOPING PUTTING CONFIDENCE

1. *Success drill: Find a straight two-foot putt. The goal is to hit 20 putts in a row from two feet and then 20 putts in a row from three feet. Focus on the images of the ball going into the hole. Watch the ball enter the hole and imprint that image in your mind. Hear the ball go into the hole. Feel the ball go into the hole. You should feel as if you can't miss.*

2. *Focused 10 drill: Hit 10 different putts on the practice green with your full preputt routine. Imagine and feel that each putt is to win a tournament. Practice your entire routine. Read the green, select and visualize a line, take practice strokes, aim and set up, and let it fire. If you become distracted or lose focus, restart your routine from the beginning.*

3. *Putting affirmations: You can use affirmations to boost your putting confidence at anytime during the day. List five affirmations that you will repeat to yourself daily. "I am a great putter and know how to make putts" and "I am a confident and composed putter and enjoy the challenge of putting" are two examples of great putting affirmations.*

---

two to four feet in length—so you can reinforce the feeling of the ball going into the hole.

THE ART OF CHIPPING AND PITCHING

Your ability to score on par 5s or save par when you are missing greens depends on how well you can pitch, chip, and putt. The short game is especially important when you don't have your "A game" and you need to scramble to make par. Why does Phil Mickelson have one of the best short games of all the players on tour? Because good chipping and pitching require strong touch and keen imagination. His superior imagination allows him to hit shots that other players wouldn't even attempt to try. He practices shots around the greens that challenge his imagination and develop his touch.

The goals of chipping and pitching practice are to control your distance, hit the ball with the correct trajectory and a solid strike, vary your practice, and increase trust. Trust is allowing your body to hit the shot without trying to produce the shot mechanically. If you have a good stroke and hit the ball solidly, you frequently can control the direction of the shot. What's more difficult to control is the distance of the shot. This requires good touch and feel, so don't use range balls when you practice chipping or pitching. They may feel and react differently from the balls you normally play with in competition. To control the distance of a chip or pitch, a player must anticipate the amount of roll or release once the ball hits the green, make a good judgment for the feel of the shot (given the trajectory and amount of spin), and execute the shot well. Half the battle is making the correct judgment of the shot you need to get it to the hole. The other half is executing that feeling with consistently good fundamentals.

These skills develop from practicing every possible shot encountered on the golf course. I ask my students to use variable-distance drills, in which they vary the distance of each shot; these are similar to the touch drills for putting. Hitting the shot with the correct trajectory is very important to controlling the spin and dis-

PATRICK'S PRACTICE DRILLS FOR PITCHING AND CHIPPING

1. *Sink it drill: Start with a 20-foot chip from just off the fringe of the green. The goal is to sink the chip in as few balls as possible. If it takes you 10 shots to make, do it again, and this time make it with fewer than 10 balls. Repeat the drill until you can sink the shot on your first try. Switch to a more difficult shot and repeat the drill.*

2. *Three cups drill: Using nine balls, find three cups on the green that line up in a straight line across the green, about 15 feet or so apart. You should have one short, one medium, and one long chip from just off the green. Hit one chip to each cup in random order. On each new chip, hit it to a different cup. Again, your focus should be on speed or pace. Repeat the drill until you can hit all nine balls within three feet of the pin.*

3. *Challenge game: This game requires a partner. Using only one ball, take turns creating a shot around the green. When it's your turn, you "call the shot" from anywhere around the green. You call the club, the type of shot, and the placement of the ball. Anything goes—the more difficult, the better. The first person to hit 10 balls closest to the hole wins.*

4. *Random pitching drill: This drill requires you to hit and to pitch to different targets. Place targets at 40, 50, 60, and 70 yards. Work your way up and down the distances alternately, never hitting the same shot twice. Use your practice swings on each shot to feel the swing needed to make a successful shot. Use golf balls you play with in competition.*

5. *Variable-trajectory drill: This drill requires you to use different clubs from the same spot off the green. Hit three balls with varying trajectories to the pin using three different clubs (i.e., hit three flop shots, three running shots, and three medium-height shots). Focus on the landing area and the trajectory of each shot. Visualize and feel each shot using your practice swing. This drill will teach you to choose which clubs give you the most consistent results for a particular shot.*

tance. Good players "see" or feel a shot they are confident they can get close to the pin. With each shot, you must determine the height of the shot, the distance the ball flies in the air, and the amount of roll after hitting the green. Good chipping and pitching require a lot of touch and imagination, but experience is also important, because it tells you how much roll or release you get with each shot.

I ask my students to hit different-height shots—by changing their clubs and type of shot, for example—from the same spot next to the green. In other words, you should practice something other than a "bread and butter" chip shot to strengthen your touch and imagination. If you normally use a sand wedge to hit a high spinning shot, try hitting a low runner with less spin. Practice playing shots with different trajectories. Each time you'll need to visualize the shot and pick a different landing spot, depending on the trajectory of the shot.

You can vary your practice in several ways. You can switch clubs, hit high and low shots, hit shots from different areas around the green, and use different techniques to practice different shots.

The last goal of chipping and pitching practice is to develop trust. Trust is the ability to let your body hit the shot without conscious interference. This is why you practice—to develop trust for when you play. The best way to develop trust is to hit shots with imagination, feel, and target awareness. To develop trust you need to involve the creative mind, not the "how to" mind. The "how to" mind wants to focus on the mechanics of the stroke.

FINAL THOUGHTS

Chapter Three discussed the importance of keeping a practice journal in which you record what you do in each lesson and what you need to work on. As part of your practice journal, you should also record what you work on each day in practice. Develop a plan or a schedule for every practice day on which you don't play (refer to the sample Four-Hour Practice Session in the box on page 53). It should outline your goals, what you want to accomplish, and what parts of the game to work on. Record goals each week in your journal and evaluate often how well you are accomplishing your goals. Revise the practice goals weekly. The practice journal can also be used to record swing thoughts you use for practice and play. Make sure to record any swing thoughts that worked well during play.

This chapter focused exclusively on how to make practice more effective. I have not mentioned practice off the golf course here, but I realize that lack of time, weather conditions, or other circumstances may not permit you to practice at the course all the time. You can supplement your on-course practice by practicing in your home, office, or hotel. Jack Nicklaus recommends that golfers take 100 swings a day in their home or backyard when they can't get to the course. If you have a smooth carpet at home or in the hotel, you can work on your putting at any time. Many of your drills can be done off the golf course, then integrated into your on-course practice. Work with your instructor to develop some off-course drills that can complement your regular practice sessions.

SAMPLE FOUR-HOUR PRACTICE SESSION FOR NONPLAYING DAYS

Putting Practice (60 minutes)

Goals: To Develop Touch, Consistent Stroke, Trust in Stroke, and Preshot Routine

1. *For 20 minutes a day, practice two or more touch drills as outlined in the box on drills for developing touch.*

2. *Practice 4–12-footers on a sloped hole. Hit putts uphill, downhill, right to left, and left to right. Start with 4 feet and move to 12 feet. Use the Three Bears Drill.*

3. *Make 10 putts with full routine to different cups on the green.*

4. *For 15 minutes practice hitting 10-foot putts on a chalk line or board. Focus on aiming skill and getting the leading edge of your putter square to the target line.*

5. *Make 20 putts in a row from 3 feet. See, hear, and feel the putt go into the hole.*

Chipping (45 minutes)

Goals: To develop speed control, improve imagination, and increase trust and confidence

1. *Sink it drill: See page 51 for instruction.*

2. *Four tees chipping drill: See page 46 for instruction; substitute chipping for putting. Focus on the feel for speed with practice strokes. To increase the difficulty of the drill, try it downhill.*

3. *Variable-trajectory drill: See page 51 for instruction.*

4. *Practice rule: Take a practice swing(s) to make a judgment and feel the distance with every chip you hit. Then execute that decision.*

5. *Practice rule: Use your full preshot routine with at least 50 percent of all chips you hit.*

6. *Practice rule: Focus on the trajectory and/or select a landing spot for each chip.*

Pitching (45 minutes)

Goals: To control distance and trajectory, develop feel, and improve confidence

1. *Place a target (towels, head covers) at 40, 50, 60, and 70 yards. Practice hitting shots to the targets in the range. With each shot, alternate distance. If possible, have someone near the targets calling out the distances of each shot for more specific feedback. (This drill may also be done by placing balls at 40, 50, 60, and 70 yards from a target in a field, such as a football field.)*

2. *Random pitching drill: See page 51 for instruction.*

3. *Use full routine (preshot routine) on last 10 shots. Focus on feeling the distance on practice swings and then executing the same feeling.*

4. *Practice rule: Take a practice swing(s) to make a judgment and feel the distance with every pitch shot you hit. Then execute that decision.*

5. *Practice rule: Vary the distance of every shot, hitting to a new target or distance.*

Full Swing (90 minutes)

Goals: To develop a consistent shot pattern, confidence, trust, and routine

1. *Use 30 minutes to work on fundamentals, practice drills, or mechanics. Focus on one goal at a time. Transfer the mechanics or drill into a feeling rather than give yourself verbal instructions. Use feedback to make sure you are doing what you want to do.*

2. *Place two parallel clubs (one for target line and one for setup line) on the ground to check alignment. Hit 20 balls to the same target to train alignment and the perception of being "square" to the target.*

3. *Play "holes" on the range. Imagine the first nine holes you will play in the next round. Pick landmarks on the range that frame each fairway and green. Use clubs you anticipate you will hit on those holes. Hit all shots with your preshot routine.*

4. *Practice rule: Play shots to different targets (using a different club for each shot), never hitting more than two balls to the same target.*

5. *Practice rule: Use full routine on at least 50 percent of all shots hit in practice.*

6. *Practice rule: Instill quality, not quantity, practice. For example, hit 50 focused shots instead of 100 shots without focus.*

7. *Practice rule: Change clubs often and use all the clubs in the bag.*

8. *Practice rule: Hit out of different lies: fairway, sand, rough, fluffy lies, etc.*

CHAPTER FIVE

MENTAL PREPARATION
FOR TOURNAMENT PLAY

Golf is a mental game. Talent and ability can take you only so far in golf; you must believe this if you want to play your best. One can't separate the mental and physical aspects of golf; both must be practiced and refined together. The process of playing a shot begins much before the start of a swing, before you place a ball on the tee, get to your ball in the fairway, or arrive at the putting green. Every shot involves making good decisions, using strong mental images and feelings, and focusing keenly on execution.

When Bob arrives at his ball in the fairway, his mind is already working. He must make several decisions as he assesses the lie of the ball and calculates the distance to the target. He evaluates many factors, such as the distance to the target, wind direction, lie, and landing area, and selects a club based on this information and his experience. Bob decides to hit a cut into the pin that is tucked on the right side of the green. But he recognizes that his target should not be the flag because of the risk of hitting his ball in a deep bunker that fronts the right side of the green. He aims for a tree behind the center of the green and mentally rehearses the shot by feeling a cut swing and visualizing the ball flying to the target. He stays focused on the target while maintaining the feeling of the cut swing. Bob sets up to the ball, aims his club, aligns his body, and gets relaxed and comfortable. Finally, he is ready to begin to swing the club, which takes less than two seconds.

Thus, the mind sets the stage for the body to produce a good golf shot. Each shot begins with several decisions, thoughts, feelings, or images and ends with the body doing exactly what it must. Bob must go through his mental and physical routine, which work in unison to produce the act of swinging the golf club. The focus of this chapter is mental preparation for tournaments and how to integrate the mental game into your practice schedule. The following five points, all of which are critical for improving your mental game, should be a part of your practice plan:

1. improving your focus in practice
2. gaining confidence via practice
3. learning to control emotions in practice
4. practicing a playing mind-set
5. developing a preshot routine

Let's take a closer look at how you can develop each of these mental skills.

BOOST YOUR FOCUS DURING PRACTICE

"What was I thinking?" you mutter in frustration after hitting a shot over the green. You lost focus for a split second and it cost you a shot, maybe two. Most players at times, lose focus, become distracted, or are too stressed to concentrate. The ability to concentrate is critical to success on the golf course; even quality practice flows from an ability to concentrate at a high level. Golf challenges your ability to concentrate, because it requires that you turn on your focus for each shot after several minutes of downtime.

Concentration is the ability to become immersed in a task without being distracted, and it involves four key elements: knowing what cues to focus on; staying focused on those cues; the ability to shift attention; and refocusing when distracted. A key to concentration is to know what's important to focus on. You must identify the task-relevant and task-irrelevant cues in golf. First, what thoughts or feelings help you make a shot? Second, what is only a distraction to that purpose? The following lists include some task-relevant and -irrelevant cues for shotmaking.

TASK-RELEVANT CUES

- today's game plan
- wind direction and strength
- distance to target
- lie of the ball
- club selection
- type of shot (fade, draw)
- pin placement
- target location
- visualization of the shot
- feeling a good shot
- practice swing(s)
- aim, alignment, setup
- affirmative self-talk
- belief in self

TASK-IRRELEVANT CUES

- the last shot
- any future shots
- tonight's party
- current score
- finishing score
- three-putt on the preceding hole
- the drive you hooked on hole 3
- playing partner's game
- spectators watching
- official's ruling on last hole

- bad break on first hole
- tough hole to come
- reachable par 5 to come
- worry about what others think

The ability to focus involves knowing what performance cues you should attend to, recognizing when you get off task, and then refocusing after you realize you're off task. First, define your preshot routine for all parts of the game (developing a focused preshot routine is discussed later in this chapter). The next skill is recognizing when you get off task by saying to yourself, "Hey, the last hole is over with. Let's get into the next shot" or something similar. Finally, you must refocus on the important cues for performing the present shot. Only the present shot matters in golf: this is the most basic notion I teach in sports psychology, but it is the hardest mental skill to achieve and apply repeatedly. You can train yourself to recognize, regroup, and refocus during practice. You must stay in the present moment and focus on the task to get the most from your practice. Thinking about the party that you'll attend after practice will not help you hit your best shot right now.

I teach players a specific preshot routine to help them focus better, among other things. One goal of a preshot routine is to focus you on performance cues, which locks your mind into the process. If you don't have a routine, your mind is free to wander as you prepare to hit a shot or putt. A routine should help you assess the course conditions, select a shot and club, and narrow your focus on execution. Your routine also locks your mind into the procedure of setup, aim, and target. If you have trouble focusing on execution, it's time for you to develop a specific preshot routine. Which I discuss later in this chapter.

First, list the steps in your routine. Rehearse your routine mentally until it's well imprinted in your mind. The time to develop a routine is in practice, not when you get on the golf course. Practice a routine for all phases of the game, and focus only on task-relevant cues when you practice. If you get distracted, catch yourself and refocus on the ingredients of your routine.

TOOLS FOR ENHANCING FOCUS

1. *A few "cue cards" will help you stay focused on the course. You can make these with index cards. Write one word or statement in color and large letters on each card, such as "Stay in the Present." These cards serve as simple reminders during the round.*

2. *Develop and practice a preround warm-up routine. Include full shots, chipping, and putting warm-up in the routine. Practice a warm-up routine once a week to familiarize yourself with it. Put your game face on during the warm-up routine. Refer to chapter 10 on developing a preround warm-up routine.*

3. *Visualize yourself playing a familiar course. The task is to play as many holes as possible without your mind wandering. The more holes you can play without distraction, the better your focus. If your mind wanders, catch yourself and refocus on the next shot.*

4. *Use the "five-minute drill" to jump-start your focus and get involved in practice. This drill requires that you engage in quality focused practice for five minutes at a time. Put all your energy into practice for the next five minutes, after which you can relax.*

CONFIDENCE DEVELOPS WITH THE RIGHT PRACTICE PLAN

Confidence can be elusive for some golfers. One day you have it and the next day it's gone. What is confidence? Confidence is the belief in your ability to play good golf—specifically, your ability to hit good shots and putts. Confidence develops from several sources, an important one being quality practice. As you develop competence in ballstriking, putting, chipping, sand shots, specialty shots, course management, and the mental game, your confidence grows.

Let's look at each of the areas of your game to evaluate your strengths and weaknesses. How would you evaluate your self-confidence on a scale of 1 (no confidence) to 10 (total confidence) in all parts of your game? In the table below, circle the number that represents your current confidence level in each of the areas.

RATING YOUR CONFIDENCE

Area of Game	Confidence Level									
Driving	1	2	3	4	5	6	7	8	9	10
Long irons	1	2	3	4	5	6	7	8	9	10
Short irons	1	2	3	4	5	6	7	8	9	10
Wedges	1	2	3	4	5	6	7	8	9	10
Pitching and chipping	1	2	3	4	5	6	7	8	9	10
Putting	1	2	3	4	5	6	7	8	9	10
Mental game	1	2	3	4	5	6	7	8	9	10
Course management	1	2	3	4	5	6	7	8	9	10
Practice habits	1	2	3	4	5	6	7	8	9	10

Let me describe the difference between playing confidence and practice confidence. Many players have high confidence in their ability to hit shots in practice but lack playing confidence. Playing confidence comes from scoring well. It's based on the ability and knowledge to get the ball into the hole.

To develop playing confidence, it's important to increase competence in the areas of your game that are lagging so you can score your best. You may be a great ballstriker, but putting may be holding you back from developing playing confidence and the ability to score. The next step is to structure your practice plan to develop the weaker parts of your game and at the same time maintain your strengths. This means giving more time and emphasis to areas in which you need to be more proficient.

A PLAN FOR DEVELOPING CONFIDENCE

1. Review the rating you gave to each area of your golf game in the table above.

2. List each part of your game, starting with the area in which you have least confidence and ending with the area in which you have the most.

3. Prioritize your practice to accommodate the areas you need to practice more than others. Focus on the specific fundamentals you need to devote more time to.

4. List the specific component skills of each part of your game, starting with the area in which you are least confident. What are the fundamental skills you have to master or improve to become better in that part of your game? For example, with putting the basics include the ability to read greens, aim, visualize, make a consistent stroke, hit the ball on line, and control speed.

CONTROLLING YOUR EMOTIONS BEFORE THEY CONTROL YOU

Why do many players begin to play progressively worse when they make one mistake? The reason is that they cannot let go of mistakes. High expectations may cause you to be judgmental of yourself and beat yourself up. When you don't play up to your expectations, frustration, anger, and dejection may be like a "monkey on the back" that follows you to the next hole and the next. By the time you let it go, the damage may already be done and you may have already made bogey or double bogey.

If a player gets upset because of hitting a poor shot on the range, I know he struggles with emotions on the course. Emotional control is a must for playing consistent golf. How often have you been frustrated after three-putting and then carried your anger with you for the next two holes? Your composure after a mistake could mean the difference between saving par and making bogey on the next hole. I can see how three-putting can make you frustrated, but even more important is how you respond afterward: your attitude can play a big part in your score on the next few holes. Emotional control is a skill you can develop off the course before you get too angry on the course to turn your anger off.

To take control of emotions, a player must first realize that external events (such as three-putting) do not automatically create negative emotions (such as frustration). Rather, it's how a player thinks about three-putting (based on personal beliefs) that causes frustration, anger, or dejection. Many of your personal beliefs such as "I must play well all the time," are irrational or self-condemning, and may become the root of emotional outbursts. They are the underlying expectations you carry with you. These beliefs often place high demands on you and subsequently your performance. For example, the belief that you should never three-putt causes you to become frustrated when you do.

The second step in controlling your emotions is to flush out irrational beliefs that lead to negative emotions. How do you know if you maintain irrational beliefs? Let's start with the basic ones. Here are five categories of irrational beliefs (adapted from Albert Ellis, 1997), along with appropriate examples:

1. Absolute demands: "I *must* play perfect all the time."
2. Awfulizing: "It's *terrible* that I made a double bogey on the last hole."
3. Self-ratings: "When I play poorly, I am *worthless* and *rotten*. I deserve to suffer."
4. All-or-nothingism: "I'm playing *either good or bad*; there's no middle ground."
5. Generalizations: "I *always* play poorly in the rain. It's raining; I'll play poorly today."

What are the beliefs you maintain about your golf game? Make a list of your irrational beliefs. The next step is to dispute—or question the validity of—each irrational belief. Here you must begin by recognizing that it's how you view an event that causes negative emotions. The next step is to expose the absurdity of your underlying beliefs. Ask yourself the following questions to help you dispute irrational beliefs:

1. What underlying belief or expectation is causing me to be so upset about what happened?

2. By holding on to this belief am I feeling better about my golf game or myself?
3. Where is the evidence that supports this belief? Is it grounded in reality?
4. Is what happened to me really that awful?
5. Is being upset really helping me to play better golf?

By disarming irrational beliefs and replacing them with a more rational philosophy, you soon realize that you have the power to control emotions. You are more in control of negative emotions after making a mistake. Instead of getting frustrated, blaming yourself, and thinking how awful it is to make a double bogey, you are able to play on with composure and patience.

The next step is to have a strategy for regaining emotional control. I've developed a five-step strategy that can be implemented in practice or anytime off the course when you feel negative emotions, such as anger, frustration, impatience, or depression. Then, when you feel one of these emotions on the course, you have a strategy ready to get past the negative emotion. The five steps are described in the box on page 66.

The goal of this strategy is to get you to stop ruminating about the mistake and to refocus on the task at hand. You can't play in the present free of emotional turmoil unless you put the error behind you.

First, recognize the negative emotion, that you are upset, and that you can change it. You are saying, "I'm in control. Let's do something positive to get under control." Second, dispute the thought that is the basis for the negative emotion. In essence, you are disputing your own beliefs and expectations. Third, calm yourself down physically. Your body gets charged up when you are emotional—think of how you feel when someone cuts you off on the highway. At this step, you can use breathing techniques, relaxation, stretching, or any other means to calm down physically. Fourth, change your thoughts to a positive emotion. This is a distraction technique to help you forget about the mistake and move on. Last, and most important, is refocusing on the task by forgetting about the mistake and getting back to playing golf one shot at a time. Every

---

FIVE STEPS TO GAINING EMOTIONAL CONTROL

1. *Recognize: Recognize the negative emotion ("I'm mad because I can't stand making bogey on a par 5").*

2. *Dispute: Dispute the belief or thought that is causing the negative emotion. ("What's so awful about making a bogey? Even the best players make bogey sometimes.")*

3. *Cool down: Cool down physically. Use breathing and stretches, tighten and release tense muscles, and slow down.*

4. *Feel positive: Change your thoughts to a positive emotion. ("It's a pleasure to play golf today.")*

5. *Refocus: Refocus yourself on the task at hand. ("What do I need to focus on to hit this shot?")*

---

step before this one is designed to help you refocus on your next shot free of negative emotion and with total composure.

You can practice this method anytime—on or off the golf course. Use it on the practice range, during a practice round, at home, in your car, or any other time you feel negative emotions. After practicing this technique, you can easily apply it to tournament golf.

A PLAYING MIND-SET BEGINS IN PRACTICE

Persistence, determination, and a strong work ethic are what drive players to practice day after day. Often, however, the same qualities that breed success for some golfers cause them to spin their wheels when they try to improve. Most perfectionistic players I work with have an extreme level of motivation. This is a great mind-set for practice day in and day out, but the same mind-set leads to unreasonable expectations on the golf course. These golfers are often great practice players who don't have playing confidence. They can't produce the same swing on the course. They may become too mechanical on the course, control their swings, try too hard, expect too much, and become frustrated when things don't go as planned.

Most perfectionistic players have learned early in life that hard work and effort are the keys to success. A perfectionist sets extremely high goals and has very high expectations. When this person fails or can't attain his goals, frustration occurs and he increases effort and determination. Soon, the player wants to succeed so badly that he fears failure and is caught in a web of anxiety. This player's goal becomes to perfect his game in practice so his swing will hold up under pressure. A perfectionistic player has to learn how to develop playing confidence in addition to confidence on the range.

Chapter Four discussed the importance of using your imagination and practicing actual golf shots instead of beating balls on the range. Perfectionists love to beat balls. If you like to practice your swing and putting stroke more than play, you may become comfortable with practice and fear playing. A practice mentality is necessary if you wish to improve, but many perfectionists I work with are stuck in swing changes and can't take their practice game to the course. One reason is that these golfers don't practice playing shots. Part of practice should be play-specific. This approach is best if you want to transfer the benefits of practice to the golf course.

The best way to make practice more play-specific is to spend more time playing on a course than at the practice range or putting green. If all you do is work on your swing, when will you ever learn how to score your best, which is the object of golf? On the course, practice is more specific to what you will encounter in tournaments.

Confidence can be elusive for a golfer who is always working on his swing and makes changes often. If you make a swing change, allow enough time to practice and ingrain the new swing. Make it repetitive instead of perfect. The challenge of making a swing change is to allow enough time to completely erase the old swing habit and ingrain the new one. Under the heat of competition, your body wants to revert to old habits. Make sure, therefore, that you practice the changes so that your swing feels repeatable before you play a match.

PRACTICE TIPS FOR GOOD MENTAL GOLF

Full Swing

1. Practice hitting shots just as you play on the course, with the same focus of mind.
2. Taper off your mechanics training two weeks before a tournament and play more golf.
3. To trigger your swing focus on one swing thought at a time.
4. Hit practice shots without any thought of mechanics. Trigger practice shots using an image of the target, an image of the shot, or a feeling of a good shot.
5. Use a full preshot routine to play shots on the range.

Putting

1. Think only about tempo or rhythm as you hit putts; don't focus on stroke.
2. See the line of the putt and let yourself respond to that image instead of trying to "stroke" the ball on a line.
3. Focus on the speed of the putt with your practice stroke and "feel" the ball to the hole.
4. Hit 20 putts with your eyes closed, focusing only on how solid the putt was.
5. Use your full preputt routine to hit putts on the practice green.

Chipping

1. Pick a spot to land the ball and focus on the height of the shot as you stroke it.
2. Look at the hole, close your eyes, and react to the image of the shot.
3. Take two or three practice swings next to the ball and feel the distance of the shot. Address the ball and repeat the feeling you just created. Use your full preshot routine to hit chips.

FIGURE 5.1

Make the practice swing an active rehearsal by focusing on the feel of the shot you intend to hit.

MENTAL PRACTICE TIPS FOR PERFECTIONISTS

1. Don't expect so much. Exceedingly high expectations can make your feel like a failure no matter what you do, and they make you judge your performance unfairly. If you don't reach your expectations, you may view your effort as a failure. Setting attainable goals for practice is a better option. Be patient as you look for improvements in your game.

2. Emphasize fun, not being perfect. You are probably very hard on yourself in practice. The tension and frustration you experience results in part from an overemphasis on trying to be perfect. Try to have fun with practice. Enjoy the time you spend practicing. Laugh at your mistakes once in a while.

3. Don't dwell on shortcomings. If you are a perfectionist, you spend a lot of time dwelling on the mistakes you make and your weaknesses. This is unhealthy for your self-confidence and doesn't let you enjoy the game. Dwelling on your weaknesses sends a message to

yourself that you are never good enough. You are not a failure—you just choose to think more about your faults. You have to make the choice to think about what you did well in practice today, remembering the good shots instead of replaying the bad shots over and over.

4. Give yourself permission to make mistakes. Perfectionists think that anything less than a flawless practice is a failure. You have to accept that you are human and that you will have bad days just like everyone else. Sometimes it helps to give yourself permission to make mistakes. You're not perfect, and even the best players in the world make mistakes. Allow yourself the flexibility to hit four or five poor shots a day.

5. Try less. Most hardworking players think that the harder they work in practice, the better they will play. Trying too hard can lead to burnout and staleness. You want to be able to play with a fresh attitude, which is hard if you are always practicing your swing and game. Take off one day a week from golf and do something else you enjoy.

6. Play as much as you practice. You don't want to get too comfortable with practice and not have the necessary confidence to play well on the course. Try to play at least as much as you practice. For every four hours of practice per week, play one round. You want to have confidence that you can hit shots on the course and not just in practice. Move your practice to the golf course whenever possible. If you can, play two balls in practice rounds.

HONE YOUR PRESHOT ROUTINES IN PRACTICE

I see players who never hit shots on the range with a preshot routine and then, on the course, go through a 45-second preshot routine. The preshot routine should be developed and honed on the range and putting green before you put it to work on the course. I believe that a preshot routine is an excellent mechanism for integrating the mental game into your play. Every player should develop a functional routine that feels good and improves consistency. When I work with players, we develop a routine that is based on sound principles of motor performance and is consistent with the player's preferences.

I have found that a consistent preshot routine can be one of a player's greatest assets. Your preshot routine should have three overall objectives: to instill confidence, to help you focus on the task, and to help set the swing into motion.

A routine should be simple and tailored to a player's preferences, yet still achieve these three objectives. A routine that is too complex makes a player focus too much on doing the routine. Whether it's for a full shot chip or a putt, your preshot routine should have the following five ingredients:

PRACTICE TIPS FOR PRESHOT ROUTINE

1. Specific plan: First you must have a specific intention of how you want to play the shot. For full shots, most good players pick a specific target (both a starting and finishing target) and the type of shot they want to hit (height, shape, and trajectory of the shot). For putting, this includes the line of the putt and the point from which you want to start the ball. For chipping, your plan should include what club to use, trajectory of the shot, distance in the air, the landing area or spot, and amount of roll of the shot. Your imagination drives your shot selection.

2. Positive image: Once you have a specific plan, program yourself with a positive image of the shot. This can be a picture, sensation, or thought of how the shot looks and how you will make it become a reality. For full shots, if you are a visual player, you will want to try to see the shot or focus on a picture of the target. A feel player should focus on the feeling of a good shot or a swing cue to trigger the swing. For putting, if you are a visual putter, you will want to see the line and the ball rolling along the line. Another good image is that of the ball rolling the last two feet before dropping into the cup. For a feel player, you should focus on feeling the speed of the putt and how much the ball will break. For chipping, visualize the trajectory of the chip and the ball rolling to the hole. If you are a feel player, you should focus on feeling the shot you want to hit and feeling the area where you want to land the ball.

3. Active rehearsal: The third ingredient of a routine is a rehearsal or practice swing, which should mirror the swing or stroke

of the actual shot or putt you plan to hit. For full shots, the practice swing helps warm up your muscles and feel the tempo of the swing needed to carry out the plan. The rehearsal is an extension of the image you have already created of the shot. An active rehearsal focuses on a swing cue; a feeling of the shot, putt, or chip; or rhythm and tempo during the practice swing or stroke. For putting, you can focus on the speed of the putt (effort control) during the practice stroke or just see the target. Focusing on tempo or a swing cue is another way to involve an active practice stroke.

4. Target or feel focus: Golf is a target game. You must have a target and align properly to that target whether visually or by feel. During the preshot routine, your focus should be on the target. The closer you get to pulling the trigger for a shot or chip, the more your focus should be on the target. For visual players, you will want to focus on the target, the shape or trajectory of the shot, or a line to the target. Feel players will prefer to focus on the feeling of a good shot or a swing cue during set up and getting ready to pull the trigger. For putting, you want to focus on the line or spot you picked earlier or you may prefer to feel the ball into the hole depending on whether you are a visual or feel player.

5. Initiate swing: A good routine allows you to trust your swing and lets your instincts take over. Here you want to trigger the swing with a simple swing cue or an image of the shot or target. Your swing should be started with either a target focus or a swing cue. You will want to test both on the range and see what brings consistency to your swing. The putting stroke should be started with a picture of the line and aiming spot, or by feeling the speed. No mechanics here. You will want to test all of them on a practice green to see what works best for you. For chipping, the swing should be started with a picture of the spot on the green and trajectory of the shot, a feeling of the speed, or a picture of the pin. Don't think about mechanics!

Test different images and feelings in each part of the routine to see what works best for you. First find out if you are more visual, kinesthetic, auditory, or a combination, by doing the following simple test: Imagine you are on the range. Experience yourself hitting balls to a target in the range. . . . Do this for 30 seconds. Now, what did you choose to focus on? Did you see yourself swinging? Did you feel the shot from inside your body? Did you focus on the sound of impact? What were the main images you used to imagine yourself swinging? Most likely, these are the images you should use in your routine. You can also tell if you are a feel or visual player by noting how the routine feels, your level of focus, the results of the shot, and the consistency of the shot when you experiment with different images. I ask my students to hit five shots with each of the following methods: focusing on the target only, feeling a good shot, and thinking about one swing cue. By observing the results and talking with the player, I can tell what works best for him. Your goal here is to find the images and feelings that help you execute the shot to the best of your ability.

The putting routine involves more feel and touch than the full swing routine. The question you need to ask is "Am I a feel, spot, or line putter, or a combination of these?" Most golfers use a combination of feel for speed and line or spot for direction. If I asked you to use your imagination to read the green, what would you do? Do you see a line from the ball to the hole? Do you see a spot on the green to roll the ball over? Or do you feel the ball turning a certain direction? Whatever images you use to read the putt, stick to those images throughout the entire routine. For example, if you are a visual player who sees a clear line to the hole, you will probably want to use that image over the ball as you initiate the stroke.

Chipping also involves more feel and touch than full shots. Most players are able to immediately visualize a shot they are most comfortable executing. They see the trajectory of the shot, where to land the ball, and how much the ball rolls after landing on the green. The trajectory of the shot will dictate the club you select. If you are a feel player, focus on the feeling of the shot and a spot to land the ball on the green. It's important in chipping to feel the line of the ball as you take practice swings. A good outcome depends on your ability to anticipate how the ball will come out of the rough (stop quickly or run hard). See the shot you want to hit including the height and roll and let that image drive your stroke.

MENTAL PREPARATION TIPS FOR TOURNAMENT GOLF

Getting to the point where you feel ready to play your best golf encompasses everything I teach in sports psychology. Feeling confident in your game, getting focused to play, being physically prepared and excited to play, and doing your homework are the keys to preparing for tournaments. Here I discuss other important factors in getting the mind ready for tournament golf.

EXCUSES TO FAIL AND REASONS TO SUCCEED

Do you create excuses why you won't play well in the next tournament? Or do you focus on the reasons why you will play your best? When I see a player who has ready-made excuses for not playing well in a tournament, I suspect he or she probably won't play well. Do you say to yourself "I hate putting on slow greens" or "I don't play well when it rains"? If you do, you think more about excuses for not playing well than about reasons why you will play well. Confident players focus on the reasons why they will succeed. Make a list of the reasons you will succeed and why you should be confident. Here are some examples:

1. I have had a great practice week.
2. I believe in my game and ability to score.
3. I'm a great putter.
4. I'm mentally tough and can handle putting on slow, bumpy greens.
5. I know the course and have studied the greens.
6. I'm driving the ball well.
7. I'm confident in my short game.
8. I'm in great shape and am stronger than ever.

Even if you think you are overstating your ability, add to your list. Most people don't give themselves enough credit. They understate their abilities and deemphasize the positive. If you deemphasize the positive, you invalidate much of your confidence. Review your list every day and remind yourself often why you should succeed.

INSIST ON NO EXPECTATIONS

Do expectations about your performance help you play well? Probably not. You can set yourself up for failure by having high expectations for your game. Replacing expectations with confidence is your best course of action here. The problem with expectations is that you place boundaries on your performance. With expectations, you presume many things, such as what you *should* shoot, how well you *should* hit the ball, how many mistakes you *should* make, and how smart you *should* play. And when you don't meet these presumptions, frustration, irritation, anger, and feelings of failure may emerge. A player may expect to shoot par every time he plays, for example. Then, when this player is four over par after nine holes, his expectation is shattered, and the round may become a case of futility—all because expectations are not being met.

Some people equate expectations with confidence. They are not the same. Confidence is the belief you can perform a task or play well, but it doesn't mean you absolutely *must* perform well. Expectations are presumptions about how well you must play to feel accomplished. Confidence helps you play better, but expectations are judgments (usually negative opinions of yourself when you don't measure up) about you and your game. As you prepare for a tournament, don't set yourself up for frustration with high expectations. Instead, focus on your ability to hit good shots and putts, one at a time.

I prefer that players use goals instead of expectations. Goals are changeable and not as absolute as expectations. You strive for your goals, but that doesn't mean you have to achieve them. Expectations are more permanent beliefs about your game; they place limits on what is acceptable and what is not. Expectations are not as flexible as goals. Goals are excellent for helping you focus on the process of execution. Have two or three process or performance goals when you play, such as number of greens hit in regulation.

FEEL RESTED AND EXCITED TO PLAY

It is possible to overtrain or overpractice, which can lead to burnout, staleness, and a lack of enthusiasm for competitive play. The best athletes in the world train hard and then decrease their training as they approach competition. Many athletes in long-distance or endurance sports, such as running or biking, have used this technique for years. In golf, you have to balance the intensity of your training with time off to refresh the mind and body. You hear stories about golfers who win tournaments after taking a week or two off because they were fresh and excited to play. The mental clutter from grinding in practice can cause you to have too many swing thoughts. Time away from practice can both help restore your body's strength and quiet your mind.

Many players on the PGA Tour play three weeks in a row and take one week off. You should set aside at least one day a week for taking a break from golf and for enjoying your family, friends, or hobbies—and don't feel guilty when you take a day off. The closer you get to competition, the less time you should spend grinding on the practice range. Some light target practice or specificity training is more appropriate the last two or three days before competition. Playing a practice round is good preparation to help quiet the mind. But that doesn't mean you should play 36 holes the day before the tournament.

FINAL THOUGHTS

In this chapter you have learned how important having a proper mind-set is in golf. The following list summarizes how to prepare yourself mentally in order to play your best:

- Identify the important cues to focus on during performance. Practice recognizing when you get off task and refocusing on the task-specific ingredients of shotmaking.
- Confidence comes from having a sound practice plan and game plan, and from your belief in your ability. Identify

the competency skills you most need to work on. Work on building up the areas of your game where you lack confidence, and also on tuning up your strengths.

- Getting control of your emotions must begin off the course. First, identify irrational beliefs that lead to negative emotions. Second, dispute those beliefs and replace them with more rational beliefs. Last, practice your five steps to regaining emotional control anytime you feel negative emotions.

- To prepare your best for tournament play, practice should be specific to what you will do on the course. Spend less time beating balls on the range and more time practicing shots of all kinds on and off the course. Play more as you approach a tournament.

- Your routine should be honed on the range and practice green. Achieve a routine that helps you focus on the task, gives you confidence, and allows you to trust your swing.

- Remind yourself every day of the reasons you have to succeed in golf. Be careful of making excuses for failure before you play.

- A lot of practice can elevate expectations. Don't expect too much of yourself on the course. Instead, have some attainable goals to shoot for and change them often.

- Too much practice can lead to burnout and staleness. Take time off from golf without feeling guilty. It will help you return to the game with a fresh body and renewed enthusiasm.

CHAPTER SIX

GETTING FIT FOR GOLF

*Not too long ago, most golfers thought that strength train-
ing was harmful to one's swing because it developed larger,
tighter muscles. But we know that's not true. The idea
behind weight training is to strengthen muscles and
joints—not just build bulk. When done correctly with
proper guidance, a weight-training program can help a
golfer can gain strength, flexibility, and joint stability. This
can lead to more energy, longer drives, and a more fluid
swing. A golfer needs these abilities to play well.*

As in any other sport, strength and flexibility are important ingredients of success in golf, and many tour pros and top amateurs now engage in regular fitness programs. One player who has
benefited from regular visits to the gym is David Duval. He started a
fitness program in 1997 and lost nearly 30 pounds. He went on to
win three tournaments in a row at the end of the 1997 season,
including the 1997 Tour Championship. He attributes much of his
continued success to this fitness program, which has helped him
maintain his new weight, get stronger, improve endurance, and get
more flexible. Duval feels that he has increased both his leg and his
arm strength considerably, which helps him hit all his clubs farther.
To date Duval has won 11 PGA Tour events and has become one of
the world's most dominant players.

Golf is one of the few sports in which most athletes work hard at developing their technique, but neglect their most vital piece of equipment—their bodies. This approach helps develop a great swing, but without a healthy body, free of injury, you won't be able to put that great swing into action. Several professional players including Dottie Pepper, Hale Irwin, Fred Couples, and Davis Love III, are now forced to stick to exercise to prevent injury and stay healthy enough to continue playing golf. In addition, all three major tours— PGA, Senior PGA, and LPGA—have full-time fitness and rehabilitation trailers at every tournament that provide the players with convenient workout and therapy facilities.

The major goals of any sport-specific exercise program should be to improve fitness and performance while decreasing the risk of injury. But there are many other, less tangible benefits to your golf game that come with improved health. An exercise program can add distance to your drives, improve concentration and energy, help protect you from stress, and increase overall flexibility, endurance, and stamina. Every spring and early summer, the USGA holds U.S. Open sectional qualifiers at various sites around the country. One is held at the Bay Hill Club in Orlando, where the players must play 36 holes in one day. In 1998, the temperature there reached 90 degrees, with a heat index approaching 100 degrees. Exercise physiology studies show that athletes who have good cardiovascular fitness respond better to intense heat environments and are better able to forestall muscular fatigue. Any golfer who has wilted coming down the stretch will tell you that you must be in shape to play 36 holes of demanding, pressure-filled golf in those conditions.

This chapter is designed to give you the knowledge to start a golf-specific exercise program—or to augment an existing program— by helping you gear it to the demands of golf. The goal here is *not* to replace an existing personalized exercise or rehabilitation program. Make no mistake: a personalized exercise program with an experienced trainer is best, because he best knows your medical history and background, goals and resources, and personal preferences. A trained instructor is also able to adapt an exercise program to reflect trouble areas, such as potentially harmful motions or habits, and maximize your benefits.

It is important that you consult with your physician before starting any exercise program, especially if you are over 40 years of age and/or have any known cardiovascular risk factors. Those with cardiovascular or orthopedic conditions should be especially cautious, and should seek proper supervision and instruction for all exercise activities. Golfers with a medical history that includes orthopedic trauma, injury, or chronic pain should undergo a complete muscular and skeletal evaluation. In addition, Paul Geisler and I recommend that you arrange for a medical authorization from an orthopedist, physical therapist, or athletic trainer prior to initiating any exercise program. More-detailed information about starting and implementing a fitness program can be found by contacting the American College of Sports Medicine at 317-637-9200, or by visiting their website at www.acsm.org.

Obviously, an exercise program is only as good as the amount of effort you expend and your commitment to the program. Every golfer has different goals, resources, and time constraints that affect his ability to commit to an exercise program. In a perfect world, we would all perform an exercise program in its entirety for five to six days per week, but our world is not perfect and many people just don't have the necessary time and resources. To get the most out of your golf exercise program, match your profile (level, goals, resources, and time) with the following exercise components and choose the program that is right for you.

PROFILE ONE (HIGHLY COMPETITIVE PLAYER):

Goals
- maximize performance and longevity
- avoid injury
- seek edge to get to next level
- improve flexibility or increase distance

EXERCISE PROGRAM — COMPLETE PACKAGE

Exercise Component	MWF	TThSa
Flexibility/mobility		•
Strength/endurance	•	
Cardiovascular		•
Practice	•	•

PROFILE TWO (COMPETITIVE AMATEUR WHO WANTS TO IMPROVE FITNESS):

Goals
- play pain free for maximum enjoyment of game
- assimilate swing changes and positions
- improve swing and scoring consistency
- add golf-specific element to current fitness program

EXERCISE PROGRAM — GOLF-SPECIFIC DRILLS ONLY

Exercise Component	MWF	TRSa
Flexibility/mobility		•
Cardiovascular	•	
Hip hinges & backswing pivots	•	•

WARMING UP BEFORE EXERCISE

Would you jump out of bed and play a full-speed game of tennis or basketball? Probably not. Neither would any successful world-class athlete. Vigorous physical activity should always be preceded by a short period of adjustment—a warm-up period—to get the body ready for action and to reduce the chance of injury. As you warm up, your heart rate, breathing rate, and body temperature increase. This causes an increase in circulation to the exercising muscles, which in turn increases the temperature of the muscles, tendons, and joint tissues. The moment you begin a warm-up, you increase the elasticity of the muscles, tendons, and ligaments and ready them for exercise.

Raymond Floyd has been known to stretch for 45 minutes prior to practicing or playing a round. Greg Norman and Mark O'Meara begin their stretching and warm-up in the hotel room before going to the course. You can do any of several activities to warm up, and it should take you 10–15 minutes, depending on your current fitness level. To be effective, a warm-up program before your regular exercise routine should have the following components:

1. Cardiovascular: The purpose of this type of exercise is to increase heart rate, blood flow to muscles and joints, body temperature, and muscle and tendon elasticity. Ten minutes on a stationary bike or a brisk walk works fine. Or you can park your car as far as you can from the clubhouse or practice facility and briskly walk to the clubhouse or range instead of parking in the closest spot. Golf is not a cardiovascular activity, but it is best to warm up the body this way if you can.

2. Flexibility and mobility: The purpose of this type of exercise is to further increase muscle, tendon, and ligament elasticity and temperature. Slowly stretch the body's major muscle groups that will be used during activity and slowly take the joints through a smooth, active range of motion. If you've ever watched professional dancers warm up, you've seen that they use slow, controlled movements to the end ranges of motion. Since golf requires you to use almost every muscle and joint in your body at some point, you need to adequately stretch and mobilize your whole body. Pay particular attention to your wrists and forearms, shoulder, torso and hips, knees, and feet; try exercises that involve joint rotation and multiple-plane movements. The exercises in the flexibility section later in this chapter are excellent warm-up exercises as well.

3. Functional exercise: The purpose of this type of exercise is to mimic the sport or activity in which you are about to participate, and it should definitely come after you have adequately stretched. In effect, these exercises ready your joints and muscles specifically for the task at hand. Swing two clubs (or a weighted club) slowly, for example, and progress from chipping to pitching and then to hitting half-shots at half speed. Work your way all the way up to full shots at full speed, with slow, controlled progression. Warming up and swinging a club left-handed (or your nondominant side) will help to ready your joints and muscles to swing at full speed.

IMPROVING CARDIOVASCULAR FITNESS

Cardiovascular exercise, or aerobic exercise, is the most important type of activity for improving overall fitness. Aerobic exercise increases the efficiency of the heart, lungs, and working muscles. Cardiovascular fitness is critical for endurance runners, but it's also very important for golfers—especially those who walk while playing. Improved cardiovascular fitness levels will increase your walking endurance and help prevent "posture fatigue" at the end of the round. Golfers in good cardiovascular shape also respond better in conditions of high heat and humidity. Paul and I recommend aerobic exercises that improve both muscular and cardiovascular endurance. Ideally, you should engage in activities that produce minimal impact and stress to the joints and bones of the legs, hips, and lower back, such as swimming, cycling, and cross-country skiing.

Aerobic exercise typically involves the use of large-muscle groups undergoing repetitive activities. To get the desired physiological benefits, you should incorporate sustained activities for longer periods of time without rest. To tax the cardiovascular and muscular systems sufficiently, the intensity of the exercise should be mild at first and then get more severe as the body adapts. The key to achieving a positive training effect and improving your cardiovascular fitness is to carefully monitor and adjust exercise frequency, duration, and intensity. Shoot for a minimum of three aerobic sessions per week, with each session

20–25 minutes in duration. For scheduling flexibility, you can also exercise five or six times per week for only 15–20 minutes and get the same benefit. Obviously, the more frequently you engage in aerobic and flexibility exercises, the more your fitness improves.

Typically, the intensity of exercise is measured by your heart rate during a workout. The goal is to work hard enough to attain a heart rate (HR) of 70–85 percent of your maximum heart rate; this is called your target heart rate. You can determine your maximum heart rate by subtracting your current age from 220 (220 − age = Estimated Maximum HR). But remember that this is only an estimate and can vary by as much as 11 or 12 beats per minute. Check with your physician for factors that may lower your heart's maximum rate, such as any medications you take, or simply ask him for your specific target heart rate.

If you are overweight, concerned about your health, or just starting out on an exercise program, you may need to keep your exercise heart rate even lower—say, 55–65 percent of estimated maximum—and gradually progress to the higher intensities as your body adapts. Your target heart rate for each exercise period should then be about 75 percent of your maximum heart rate (Target Heart Rate = Estimated Maximum HR times 75%). Thus, if you are 40 years old, your max heart rate is 180 beats per minute. Seventy-five percent of 180 is 135—this would be your target heart rate.

Whatever your target heart rate, your perceived level of exertion—or how strenuous the exercise feels to you—is a good indicator of your intensity. Use this as a smart guide or personal barometer of the intensity of exercise. If exercise feels too strenuous to continue for the entire duration, reduce the intensity, and vice versa. Remember, exercising in high heat and humidity increases the difficulty and stress on your system, so exercise at lower intensities until you have acclimated to the environment and are ready to increase the intensity. The acclimatization process usually takes seven to ten days to complete, depending on your initial fitness level. Also remember to thoroughly hydrate yourself before, during, and after exercising in hot environments by drinking more water than you think you need (eight 8-ounce glasses of water per day).

To get an aerobic benefit, your goal should be to maintain a target heart rate during aerobic exercise for at least 15–20 minutes. This does not include your five-minute warm-up and your short cool-down period. If you exercise five or more times a week, 15 minutes is beneficial. If you exercise three times a week, 20 minutes or longer is sufficient. You can do a variety of aerobic exercises that fit your lifestyle. Walking is considered aerobic exercise (you burn the same number of calories walking and running one mile) if you achieve your target heart rate, which for some people may be difficult to do. The other option is to walk for longer periods of time (i.e., 45–60 minutes). Swimming, biking, and running are popular forms of aerobic exercise. If you have had orthopedic problems in your legs or spine, you should engage in low-impact exercise that minimizes the forces and stress on joints.

If you are a member of a local gym, there may be exercise machines available there for use, including Stairmaster, Lifecyles, Cardio-Glide, HealthRiders, and Upper Body Ergometer machines, which are excellent for any golfer. All low-impact, cardiovascular training devices are excellent tools for exercise, but remember to start slowly and increase the workload gradually.

IMPROVING MOBILITY AND BALANCE

A full golf swing places large amounts of stress, over very short time periods, on the average golfer, so proper joint mobility, flexibility, and balance are key to achieving and maintaining a successful golf swing. The following exercises are designed to improve posture, maximize shoulder and hip mobility, enhance balance, and decrease spinal stress.

1. Hip-hinge drill: This drill promotes proper posture and lowers spinal stresses (see Figures 6.1a and 6.1b).

The following exercise, called the hip-hinge drill, will help you achieve a proper primary spine angle. To obtain and keep a correct setup posture, perform this exercise for 10–15 minutes every night in front of a mirror until it becomes fluid and automatic for you.

FIGURE 6.1a

The hip-hinge drill. Start standing in neutral and work into your setup position without letting your back leave the shaft of the club. Return to starting position by staightening your legs and unhinging.

FIGURE 6.1b

The hip-hinge drill

a. Stand tall, holding a 3-iron along your back from head to buttocks. Hold the club high and low, as shown in Figure 6.1a.

b. Perform a hip hinge by keeping your back straight and flexing the hips and knees simultaneously so that your chest is lowered over the ball/floor. You should feel as though you are bringing your sternum over and between the balls of your feet, balanced and stable.

c. The club should not leave the back throughout the exercise. If it does, you are either flexing your upper spine or arching your lower spine.

d. Return to the erect starting position by straightening your legs and unhinging at the hips simultaneously. All of the effort should be focused in your legs, not your spine.

2. Backswing rotation drill: This drill increases your rotation and decreases spinal stress. Proper execution of this drill will improve your spinal mobility and mechanics by helping you maintain your secondary spine angle. (See Figures 6.2a and 6.2b.)

a. Start from your normal setup position and rotate to your backswing. Move your shoulders first and then let your hips rotate. Feel your shoulders pulling your hips to the top of the backswing. Perform 20 repetitions.

3. Hula-hoops: This drill improves hip mobility.

a. Stand with your feet together; begin making small clockwise circles with your hips, while keeping your feet and knees as still as possible. Make the circles as small and tight as possible, and feel the work your feet are actually doing. Reverse to counterclockwise direction. Perform 100 repetitions in each direction.

b. Stand with your feet about shoulder width and repeat the above exercise 100 times in each direction.

4. Chicken wings: This drill improves shoulder mobility and posture.

a. Start with your hands together in front of you, as shown in Figure 6.3a, and begin by raising your shoulders and

FIGURE 6.2a

Backswing rotation drill. Be sure not to move your hips and legs too early in the rotation—or too much. Feel as though your shoulders are pulling your hips to the finish position.

FIGURE 6.2b

Backswing rotation drill

FIGURE 6.3a

Chicken wing drill. Don't arch your back. Perform slowly and deliberately by actively "squeezing" the muscle in your upper back and shoulder blades.

FIGURE 6.3b

Chicken wing drill

FIGURE 6.3c

Chicken wing drill

arms so that your hands are raised above your head as shown in Figure 6.3b.

b. With your arms above your head, simultaneously squeeze your elbows backward as if you could touch them behind you, rotate your hands backward as if you were going to cock both arms to throw, and gradually squeeze your elbows down as if you were attempting to tuck your elbows into your back pockets, as shown in Figure 6.3c. Finish by bringing your hands back together in front of your waist.

c. Don't allow your lower back to arch. Motion should be performed slowly, with rhythmic contractions of all of your back and shoulder muscles throughout.

d. Perform 15 repetitions, twice a day. Also try this while seated in your office or kitchen chair during the day, but be careful not to arch your spine when trying to get your arms down into your back pockets.

5. One-legged golf swings: This drill improves balance and hip mobility (see Figure 6.4).

    a. Stand on your back-side leg (the right for a right-handed golfer), get your balance, and fold your arms across your chest. Using your pelvis, slowly rotate your hips toward the backswing side and return to your neutral starting position. Go as far as you can without losing your balance at any time during the motion. Gradually increase speed as you maintain your balance.

    b. Repeat with your left leg, this time turning from neutral into the finish position and back.

    c. Progress to doing this exercise with your eyes closed, then on a two-by-four block (1 foot long) with your eyes open, then with your eyes closed.

FIGURE 6.4

One-legged golf swings. Rotate slowly with balance. Move with control so that you don't fall over. This drill improves balance and coordination.

IMPROVING FLEXIBILITY

Flexibility is very important for golfers, especially those with poor posture, inactive players, players with chronic injuries, and older players, since everyone typically loses flexibility with age. Perform all flexibility exercises for 3–5 repetitions and hold each for 5 to 10 seconds. Don't be afraid to move slowly and add subtle motion to your exercises—the body is designed to move. But don't bounce in and out of the exercise, because the muscles won't relax. Make sure to breathe and relax; the idea is to get the muscles and tendons to release. Don't tense up your muscles and tendons until they hurt, because they won't relax this way either. Make gains in flexibility over a period of one to two weeks rather than daily, and never attempt to achieve the range of motion of other people. Your genetics, posture, activity, and growing patterns have a large influence on your flexibility levels.

1. Supine hamstring stretch: Use this drill for proper hip hinge position, for hip rotation, and for relieving lower-back stress (see Figure 6.5).

   a. Lie on your back with one leg flexed 90 degrees at the hip and 90 degrees at the knee, and your opposite leg extended straight on the floor.

   b. Grasp behind your flexed thigh with your hands and try to straighten your knee slowly without moving your thigh. Hold for 20 seconds and relax. Repeat by rotating your foot inward and outward, to isolate the different hamstring muscles, before extending your leg.

2. Lying crossover: This exercise improves hip, leg, and lower-back rotary flexibility for golfers having difficulty keeping their lower body quiet (see Figure 6.6).

   a. Lie on your back with your left leg straight. Bend your left knee and grasp it with your right hand, keeping both shoulders flat. Extend your left arm straight away from your body on the floor.

   b. Gently pull the bent knee to the opposite shoulder while keeping the opposite leg and shoulders still. Switch legs and repeat.

FIGURE 6.5

Supine hamstring stretch. This is a great drill for isolation of each muscle.

FIGURE 6.6

Lying crossover drill

3. Pelvic rock 'n' rolls: This exercise enhances rotary flexibility of lumbar spine and hips for those golfers having trouble with hip rotation and keeping back-side knee flexed during backswing (see Figures 6.7a and 6.7b).

a. Lie on a firm surface with your knees and hips bent, your feet and hips touching each other. Your toes should be up so that your heels are touching and are being used as a pivot point.

b. Slowly rotate your knees and hips to one side, pulling down with the bottom-side hand and going as far as you can without discomfort. Hold the stretch with your bottom hand for three repetitions to each side. Then rock 'n' roll from side to side with continuous slow motion, keeping your shoulders and chest quiet. Continue for one minute.

FIGURE 6.7a

Pelvic rock 'n' roll drill. Move from side to side with continuous slow motion, while keeping your shoulders and chest still.

FIGURE 6.7b

Pelvic rock 'n' roll drill

4. Cat stretch: This stretch improves flexibility of upper torso, rib cage, and arms for those having difficulty with swing width/ length and keeping lead elbow straight (see Figure 6.8).

    a. Get on all fours with your buttocks toward the heels, keeping your back straight.

    b. With one arm, extend your hand out and anchor it onto the floor. Press the heel of your hand down and slowly sit back on heels, keeping your hand stationary. Push your ribs and hips to the same side, then rotate your opposite shoulder underneath your stretched side. Experiment with different angles with this stretch.

5. Backswing stretch with club: This stretch improves mobility and elasticity of shoulder complex to improve swing width and length, and helps keep left elbow still (see Figure 6.9).

    a. Grasp grip end of club with the palm of your lead hand facing skyward. Place bottom hand above the clubhead,

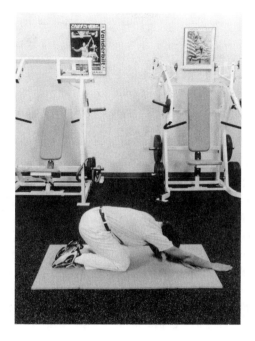

FIGURE 6.8

The cat stretch. Using one arm at a time, extend hand above head and anchor onto floor. Press the heel of your hand down into the mat or ground and slowly sit back on your heels, keeping your hand stationary.

FIGURE 6.9

Backswing stretch with club

palm facing down. Cross over your hands and arms as shown.

b. Keeping lead elbow straight, gradually go into your backswing position and push with your bottom, backside hand toward the sky. You should feel a stretch in the back of your lead shoulder. Be sure to rotate your torso.

6. Corner stretch: This stretch improves flexibility of the front of the chest and shoulders.

a. Stand facing the corner with your arms elevated about 90 degrees and your elbows flexed 90 degrees. Your feet should be together and your torso should be straight.

b. Place your forearms flush against the wall and gradually lower yourself into the corner as a straight unit. Do not arch or slouch your back. Be sure to keep your head up, and relax your shoulders and chest.

7. Lag stretch: This stretch helps to develop and increase external rotation of your back-side shoulder to create more lag on downswing and allow more freedom to swing on plane (see Figure 6.10). Do not perform this exercise if you have shoulder problems!

a. Stand with your right arm out to the side 90 degrees and your elbow level with shoulder; place the head of a club in your hand with the shaft behind your elbow and pointing toward your feet.

b. Pull down on the club with your opposite hand while keeping the elbow level until you feel a stretch in the anterior shoulder. Do not arch your back or lower your arm. Discontinue this stretch if it causes any shoulder discomfort.

8. Office stretch: This stretch increases rotary flexibility of your neck and shoulders without allowing your hips and legs to move (see Figure 6.11).

a. Sit on the edge of a stable chair in a good, erect posture, with your feet flat on the floor.

b. Rotate your shoulders around to the right and grab hold of the chair. Hold your position and then reverse motion to the other side.

FIGURE 6.10

The lag stretch. Do not do if you have shoulder problems! Slowly pull forward on the bottom of the club to increase the stretch to the anterior of your shoulder.

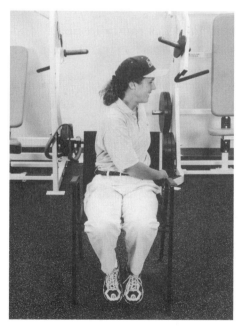

FIGURE 6.11

The office stretch

FIGURE 6.12

The address stretch. Rotate to the backswing side, using the club as a lever. Use the front elbow to help push you. Try to imitate your actual swing.

9. Address stretch: This stretch improves rotary flexibility and mobility of the hips and spine in a functional backswing position (see Figure 6.12).

    a. Stand in the address position with a long club threaded behind your lower back and your feet rotated neutral to outward. Remember to keep your spine angle consistent throughout the exercise.

    b. Rotate to the backswing side, using the club as a lever. Use the front elbow to help push you. Reverse action to the follow-through side. Remember to imitate your actual swing.

IMPROVING STRENGTH AND ENDURANCE

The following exercises can be done at home, in the office, or on the road. They simply require you to gradually increase the number of repetitions and pay attention to technique. Each exercise addresses specific weak points and areas of vulnerability for chronic problems and will benefit all golfers who employ them correctly.

　1. Sit-ups: If you have a back condition, please seek medical clearance or supervision before doing any type of sit-ups. Proper abdominal control and endurance are critical for providing trunk stability and preventing lower-back problems (see Figure 6.13).

  a. Lie on an exercise mat or carpeted floor, your hips and knees bent so your feet are flat on the floor. Beginners should place their arms across the chest; those with better abdominal control can place their hands on their ears.

  b. Rotate your pelvis so that your lumbar spine feels comfortable and neutral. Contract your abdominal muscles to hold your pelvis and spine in this position throughout the entirety of this exercise. This is a pelvic brace. Do not flatten or arch your back to maximum levels.

FIGURE 6.13

Sit-ups

    c. Slowly lift your shoulders and head off the floor until the bottom portion of your shoulder blades leaves the floor. Then slowly return to your previous position without relaxing your abdominal musculature. Make sure that your lower spine is not arching and flattening as you raise and lower your upper body. The pelvic brace should prevent this.

    d. Let quality be your guide: when you begin to fatigue, stop and rest for 30 seconds before continuing.

    e. Start with three sets of 15–20 repetitions and progress to 100 a day.

2. Seated abdominal oblique: The spine is forced to rotate at high speeds during the golf swing, and the oblique muscles of the abdomen are responsible for rotating your torso, and protecting it from unnecessary stresses (see Figure 6.14a and 6.14b).

    a. Sit on the edge of a flat-bottomed, stationary chair with your feet flat on the ground. Rotate your pelvis so that it is in a neutral, correct posture. Don't slouch or arch. Slightly retract your shoulders so your ears line up with your shoulders.

    b. Fold your arms across your chest and begin by rotating to the backswing side and then back to neutral. The motion should be short, tight, and fairly rapid. Think of twisting your belly button to the right and then to the left. Do this for 30 seconds, and repeat three times.

    c. Perform the same exercise to the follow-through side. Be sure to maintain your original posture throughout the entire motion, and to keep your head still. You can make this exercise more difficult by holding a 5- to 10-pound dumbbell on your chest.

3. Prone rotator cuff exercises: The lead shoulder, in particular, is very vulnerable to overuse stress and dysfunction with habitual ballstriking over long periods of time. Rotator-cuff endurance and proper function are critical if you wish to avoid nagging shoulder pain.

FIGURE 6.14a

Seated abdominal oblique

FIGURE 6.14b

Seated abdominal oblique

a. Lie facedown on a firm bed or exercise table for all these exercises. Hang the exercising arm over the edge so that it is free to move.

b. Begin using a 1- to 2-pound dumbbell, or cuff weight, and *never* use more than five pounds for this exercise.

c. Raise the arm, with the thumb up, straight over your head and back slowly (see Figure 6.15a).

d. Raise the arm, with the thumb up, straight out to the side and back slowly (see Figure 6.15b).

e. Raise the arm, with the thumb out and back, straight back and return slowly (see Figure 6.15c).

f. The arc of motion for these exercises should be short, smooth, and controlled.

g. Perform exercise c, rest 30 seconds, perform exercise d, rest 30 seconds, then perform exercise e. Then rest two–three minutes and repeat this sequence two or three times for each shoulder, two or three times a week.

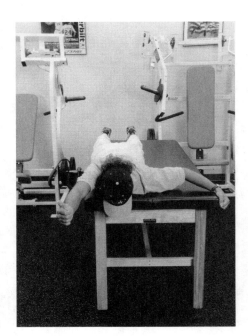

FIGURE 6.15a

Prone rotator cuff exercise

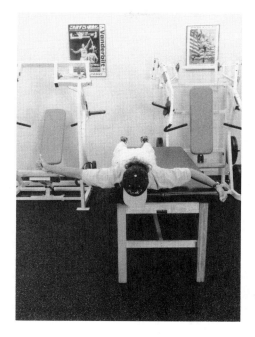

FIGURE 6.15b

Prone rotator cuff exercise

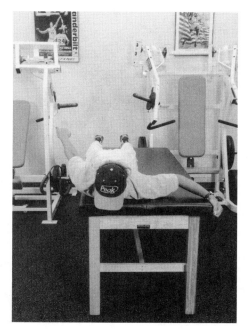

FIGURE 6.15c

Prone rotator cuff exercise

4. External rotation with tubing: (See Figure 6.16.)
   a. Stand facing a mirror in good pelvic and scapular posture (slightly retract your shoulders so your ears line up with your shoulders). Hold tubing (available at most physical therapy clinics and gyms) in your hand with a towel roll underneath your exercising elbow, your hand at your belly button, and your thumb pointing upward.
   b. Without moving your torso or your upper arm, slowly rotate your hand and move your forearm outward and away from your body's midline. Return slowly to the original starting position.
   c. Repeat 15 times, three sets for each shoulder.

5. Close-handed push-ups: This exercise is excellent for improving shoulder strength and stability needed to produce club-head speed and avoid injury (see Figure 6.17).
   a. Perform push-ups with your hands turned inward so that the fingers point at each other. Focus on a slow, controlled downward motion.

FIGURE 6.16

External rotation with tubing

FIGURE 6.17

Close-handed push-ups

b. Repeat 15 times, and repeat for three or four sets.

6. Dynamic rowing: This exercise can be performed with dumbbells or standing with tubing. Excellent for improving upper-back and shoulder posture and to counteract the effects of gravity and overuse of the arms (see Figure 6.18).

a. Stand and hold tubing in both hands, with tubing attached to a door handle or other fixed object about chest height. Be sure to have good posture with scapular retraction (pull your shoulder blades back together). Hands should start together in front of you, with your thumbs pointing inward or down.

b. Pull your arms back, keeping the elbows shoulder height. Another variation of this exercise is rotating your thumbs outward simultaneously, and retracting the shoulder blades. Keep your arms as close to your body as possible. Hold end position for a two count and slowly return to

FIGURE 6.18

Dynamic rowing

starting position, making sure to extend and reach for a full range of motion.

c. Perform 15 repetitions, times three sets.

7. Wrist roll-ups or curls: This exercise is very effective for prevention or alleviation of golfer's elbow symptoms, which is discussed in Chapter Seven (see Figures 6.19a and 6.19b).

   a. Seat yourself as pictured. Extend one arm parallel to the floor, the other hand supporting the extended arm at the elbow. Using the extended arm with the palm facing down, curl your wrist upward while holding a weight in your hand. Raise the weight upward to flexed position. Reverse and roll the weight back down. The elbows should not bend and the shoulders should not move during this exercise.

   b. Begin with two–four pounds and progress to six–eight pounds and perform five–seven repetitions with two–three minutes of rest between sets.

FIGURE 6.19a

Wrist curls

FIGURE 6.19b

Wrist curls

    c. Repeat exercises a and b this time with your palms facing upward.

  8. Dumbbell flies: The pectoral muscles are very active in producing arm speed—and therefore clubhead speed. Increasing the function and strength of these muscles will help produce more natural clubhead speed from your upper body.

    a. Lie on your back on a flat exercise bench with your elbows bent approximately 90 degrees and dumbbells in your hands.

    b. Slowly lower your elbows and hands to the floor, then press them upward, attempting to round your chest, so that your hands meet in the midline of your body as high up as possible without leaving the bench. Slowly lower and repeat.

    c. Begin with 15–20 pounds and perform three sets of 15 repetitions. Progress in weight but stay with high repetitions and low weight for endurance and range of motion.

  9. Lat pull-downs: The latissimus muscles are also very active in producing arm speed—and therefore clubhead speed (see Figure 6.20).

    a. Begin seated at a pull-down machine with your hands as wide apart as possible without causing discomfort. Sit in good posture and in a position so that your head won't be in the way.

    b. Maintaining spinal neutrality and control, slowly pull down in front of your face to about collarbone level, then slowly return with control.

    c. Perform 15 repetitions for three sets. Begin with a weight you can handle for this many repetitions and progress as needed. A good starting place for most people is 25 to 35 percent of your body weight.

HELPFUL HINTS FOR YOUR EXERCISE PROGRAM

- Start exercise with a 5- to 10-minute warm-up and end with a 5-minute cool-down.
- Always stretch before and after lifting weights.

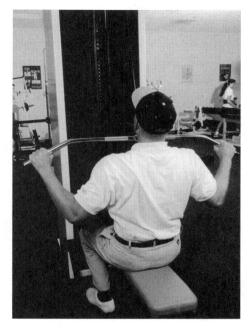

FIGURE 6.20

Lat pull-downs

- Immediately before you lift weights, try performing your cardiovascular exercise to thoroughly warm your body up.
- Lift weights three times a week per muscle group, with a day of rest in between.
- Work larger muscle groups before smaller ones (chest muscles before triceps, triceps before forearms, etc.).
- Start with light to moderate weights and perform more repetitions. Avoid heavy weights with fewer repetitions.
- As you develop your muscles, you can gradually increase the number of sets and repetitions, and, when you feel comfortable, increase the weight.
- To avoid losing any range of motion, always use a controlled movement with all weight-training exercises.
- Eat a proper, well-balanced diet. Eat enough foods to fuel your exercise needs.

FINAL THOUGHTS

Be sure to start out slowly and gradually increase the intensity and volume of all exercises you do. You can benefit from all these exercises, but only if you do them properly and in the proper doses. This exercise program is not a substitute for expert supervision. Don't attempt any exercise that you are not comfortable with, and use common sense—if it hurts, discontinue and seek medical attention as soon as possible.

CHAPTER SEVEN

PLAYING INJURY-
AND PAIN-FREE GOLF

*Golf is very much a physical game that can cause severe
physical injuries. Just ask Scott Verplank, Lee Trevino, or
Beth Daniel. As a result of injuries to these players and others, today all professional golf tours have full-time fitness
and rehabilitation facilities on-site at tournaments. These
fitness centers are staffed with physicians, physical therapists, athletic trainers, and the latest fitness and rehabilita-
tive equipment. In addition, many professional golfers now
use personal fitness trainers to help them improve strength
and flexibility, and to prevent injury. Notables such as Tiger
Woods, David Duval, Greg Norman, Mark O'Meara, Jim
Colbert, and Nancy Lopez are just some of the players who
use personal trainers to improve their fitness and performance levels.*

Casual observers of the game may think that golf does not require
much physical skill or athletic ability. However, any experienced
golfer knows that you need strength, agility, coordination, and
endurance to play well. Great players like Ernie Els and Annika
Sorenstam have fluid and simple-looking swings, but don't be fooled
into thinking that a full swing is not stressful to the body. No matter
how graceful, slow, or accurate a swing looks, it's a very fast and

complex motion that produces high levels of stress in the joints and muscles of even the most fit and efficient golfer.

Fred Couples, Davis Love III, and Ernie Els share the same physical therapist, who takes care of their backs using highly specialized treatments and exercises. In fact, they often bring the physical therapist to tournaments. Tour pros make golf look easy, but the golf swing requires considerable repetition and craftsmanlike precision to produce accurate results. The speed of the golf swing and the torque it creates can easily lead to physical injury. Therefore, physical conditioning and efficient swing mechanics are of paramount importance in maximizing performance and minimizing injury for every golfer.

Take the case of a talented and successful LPGA teaching professional from the Northeast named Penny. After playing in constant pain for a year, Penny was forced to stop practice and play because of a debilitating rib and midback injury. Fourteen medical doctors and specialists evaluated her, and none could find a specific mechanism for the injury or even a definitive source of her pain. She was confused, and because she was possibly facing the end of her competitive playing career, her frustration mounted.

An evaluation of Penny's physical abilities, injury history, and swing motion revealed that her poor swing biomechanics, combined with significant muscle weakness and poor stability in her upper body and trunk strength, were the culprits. Her full golf swing, although it had been productive for her for years, was mechanically inefficient and had put a large amount of stress on the left front rib cage and midspine areas, simultaneously causing spinal dysfunction. Lack of adequate muscle strength and endurance in her arms, shoulders, and torso had prohibited her from absorbing and dissipating the high repetitive forces of the swing. It was just a matter of time before pain and injury began to affect her mental well-being, playing level, and overall enjoyment of the game.

The best treatment for Penny was selective rest (avoidance of the full golf swing and any other activities that caused discomfort). Then aggressive upper-body strengthening, golf-specific flexibility exercises, and a full swing overhaul were necessary to restore a healthy golf game. Her athletic trainer consulted with her instructor to help him construct a new golf swing—one that would produce accurate results without placing undue physical stress on her body. Penny's golf teacher taught her a new swing that was more biomechanically sound than her old one, and her athletic trainer monitored her practice routine. After rest, the building of a more efficient swing, and improvements in her physical ability to absorb stress, she successfully returned to competitive play.

THE REALITY OF GOLF INJURIES

Have you ever stopped playing or practicing because of physical discomfort, pain, or injury? Most players know that golf is a difficult enough challenge even if you are healthy and free of pain. Aside from causing you to play bad golf, the pain and discomfort from an injury can ruin the enjoyment of the game and all it offers. It may surprise you to discover that injuries cause professional golfers to lose, on average, more than five weeks of playing time a year.

Tour pros hit hundreds of golf balls every day, and compared to athletes in other sports, they have a very short off-season to rest and recuperate. This increases their susceptibility to acute musculoskeletal failure and several chronic overuse injuries. Research data indicates that approximately 90 percent of Tour professionals get injured playing golf and that one-third of these players continue to play. Looked at another way, this figure means that approximately 35 players in any given full-field tournament (144 players) are playing injured. Obviously, this negatively affects their playing and performance potential.

What kinds of injury do the game's elite suffer from? Centinela Hospital, which used to manage the PGA and Senior PGA Tour Fitness Vans, reported injury rates on the PGA and Senior PGA Tours from 1990 to 1994 (Centinela Hospital, 1995). These findings are summarized in the table on page 116.

Club professionals are not immune from golfing injuries either. Reports have shown that 85 percent of club pros have been injured playing golf, with each player averaging two injuries during his professional career (McCarrol and Gioe, 1982). Much like their professional touring counterparts, club professionals most commonly

PGA TOUR AND SENIOR PGA TOUR INJURY RATES

Type of Injury	Percentage
Back	50
Shoulder	8
Hand	7
Elbow	6
Foot	6
Wrist	6
Neck	5
Other	12

suffer injuries to the left wrist, lower back, and left hand. Female professional golfers have more hand injuries than men do, whereas men have more back injuries than women. These differences are most likely due to differences between the sexes in hand and upper-extremity strength, and lower flexibility in the legs and spine. Spinal dysfunction, intervertebral disk degeneration, fractures, tendinitis, ligament sprains, muscle strains, and other fatigue-related injuries are the most common injuries among competitive golfers.

Although they play and practice less, amateur golfers are also susceptible to injuries. Researchers in Great Britain (Batt, 1992) found that nearly half of all amateur golfers get injured directly, or experience pain, while playing golf. Furthermore, it was found that about one-third of all reported injuries occur during play or practice. Preexisting injuries can also affect a golfer's health and performance by causing what the authors termed "indirect injuries." Overall, nearly half of the injuries among amateur golfers are back related, ranging from lumbosacral strains to herniated disks (Hosea and Gatt, 1996). As in the general population, many of the back problems seen among amateur golfers result from chronic wear and tear on the stabilizing structures of the spine. Poor posture and lack of physical conditioning also take their toll over the years.

Even among amateur golfers, the golf swing is capable of generating enough force to cause acute, traumatic fractures, strains, sprains, and spinal disk damage. Injuries may occur in the hand and wrist, the elbow, the shoulder, and the knee. Failure to warm up properly, too much play or practice, poor fitness levels, and poor swing mechanics are the most common causes of injury among amateur golfers today.

INJURY PATTERNS

What are the most common golf injuries and the mechanisms for injury? Every injury has its own set of circumstances and factors that contribute to its severity, complexity, and symptoms. To best assess your potential for injury or an existing problem you might suffer from, a complete investigation of your history, signs, and symptoms and an analysis of your swing pattern is necessary. Here I will highlight some common patterns in the injuries seen among golfers today.

It is important to note that many injuries in a sport like golf start out as "harmless" aches or pains, then worsen because of improper attention and treatment. To minimize your risk of significant injury, learn to listen to your body. When actual tissue damage occurs, the body begins a complex chemical cycle that results in edema (swelling) and pain. Swelling can begin at places within the joint that you can't see or feel, but you can feel the pain that accompanies fluid buildup. This is the process that usually kick-starts many chronic overuse injuries. The earlier this irritation-swelling-pain cycle is broken, the less severe the injury and the quicker the recovery.

Muscle ache that occurs within 24 to 48 hours after intensive, unaccustomed activity usually indicates a rather benign condition known as "delayed-onset muscle soreness." Most of us have felt this ache after starting an exercise program, after helping someone move heavy items, or just after overdoing practice one day on the driving range. The condition usually disappears within 72 hours and generally does not reoccur as long as activity level does not change significantly.

If you experience pain near the joints of the long bones that increases after activity and diminishes as your body warms up, you might be experiencing tendinitis. Typically, tendinitis causes soreness a few hours after exercise, makes you feel very stiff and sore in the early-morning hours, and improves when you begin to move and stretch the involved tendon(s). Prolonged, untreated tendinitis can lead to what is known as "fatigue failure," where the tendon ruptures after periods of long-term swelling and stress. This commonly occurs in the shoulders, elbows, and ankle joints.

Sharp, persistent pain in specific places within muscles, tendons, or joints usually indicates that some sort of injury has occurred. Other signs of significant injury to watch for are an inability to move a joint through its full range of motion, numbness or tingling, burning and radiating pain, and abnormal and obvious swelling or discoloration. The best rule to follow is "better safe than sorry." Check with your physician if any pain or symptom lasts more than 48 hours.

MECHANICAL LOW-BACK DYSFUNCTION

Much like the average person, many golfers suffer from lower-back dysfunction and pain that in most cases can be attributed to repetitive movement and faulty swing mechanics. Genetics, poor physical conditioning, poor posture, spinal instability, muscular weakness, poor body mechanics, and poor flexibility can lead to long-term stress to the muscles, ligaments, bones, and spinal disks. Many laypeople think that rotation of the spine is the primary or sole culprit of back dysfunction. In fact, rotation is the best way to increase blood flow and nutrition to your intervertebral disks. The spine is actually most at risk from a combination of the rotation, lateral bending, and hyperextension that occur during the full golf swing.

The best way to minimize your risk of sustaining nagging or debilitating back discomfort is to develop an efficient golf swing. By that I mean a swing that maintains both spine angle positions (see "A Healthy Setup and Address Position," later in this chapter—the angles your spine and trunk form when looked at face-on, and down-by-the-line views) and avoids reverse pivots, reverse-C's, and excessive lateral motion. In fact, by following this advice you can decrease 50–80 percent of the stress on your spine every time you swing. This is best accomplished by maintaining spinal stability and a natural motion, and staying in good shape (see Chapter Six) with specific back, trunk, and postural exercises.

GOLF SWING FAULTS TO AVOID

A reverse-C occurs when a golfer slides the hips forward during the downswing, resulting in a "C" position of the spine at impact with head well behind the lower body at the finish. This places a lot of stress on the spine, which can lead to pain and in many cases injury. The reverse-C position is the most common golf swing fault and the primary cause of lower-back injury.

The reverse pivot is the opposite of the reverse-C. The reverse pivot occurs when the lower body shifts away from the target while the head stays stationary, resulting in the spine tilting toward the target at the top of the backswing. The body must compensate on the downswing to return to its original tilted position.

HOOK OF HAMATE FRACTURES

The hamate is a small, irregularly shaped bone with a small protruding hooklike structure extending into the lower-palm space of your wrist. It lies under the "fat pad" of the palm on the pinky side of the hand. In the typical golf grip, the hook presses directly on the butt of the club, placing unnecessary stress on the bone during the downswing and impact. Violent impacts involving a steep angle of attack and deep divots can cause the hook to fracture off the main bone.

Another concern with the hamate bone is the ulnar nerve. This nerve passes right by the hamate and can easily be irritated by a fractured hook, producing sharp, burning pain (neuritis) in the ring and little fingers. A lot of practice from driving range mats can cause this problem, so golfers who practice exclusively on these mats should be cautious. Surgery is usually the only way to correct hook of hamate fractures.

Ulnar Ligament Impingement Syndrome

On the pinky side of your hand, the end of your ulnar bone connects with the small carpal bones of the wrist. In the adjoining space are several small, vulnerable ligaments that stabilize this mobile joint. As the hands and club release near impact, the ligaments of the lead hand (the left in a right-handed golfer) are pinched and compressed at a very high speed between the end of the ulna (styloid process) and the wrist bones (carpal bone). Hitting balls off hard surfaces and repetitive irritation from prolonged play and practice can increase the stress placed on these tissues. This can lead to irritation, pain, and eventual wrist joint dysfunction if left untreated. Unfortunately, not much can be prescribed for this condition except selective rest.

About 10 percent of the population is born with abnormally long ulnar bones, which may extend farther into this joint space. As you might expect, this condition increases susceptibility to the impingement syndrome, since less stress and fewer full swings are needed to initiate the pain-dysfunction cycle. If you experience pain in this area of your wrist, an x-ray is the only way to tell if you have an abnormally long ulnar styloid process. Chronic, long-term dysfunction caused by this condition can be corrected only with surgery to trim the ulnar styloid process.

Golfer's Elbow

Most golfers have some experience with golfer's elbow. Golfer's elbow and tennis elbow are actually the same thing, caused by different sports. You may see golfers practicing or playing with compressive straps on their elbows to relieve stress. Players such as Scott

Verplank, Bill Glasson, and Dana Quigley have used these straps to treat golfer's elbow.

Much like the hands, a golfer's elbow is highly susceptible to injury because of its relative frailness and poor ability to handle repetitive stress. Golfers can sustain muscle tears (strains) and tendinitis in the inside or outside of either elbow joint. Golfers who swing on plane and bow the lead wrist just prior to impact can overstretch the lateral extensor muscles of the left forearm. Golf swings that require excessive supination at impact in order to square the club also increase stress on the lead elbow.

In contrast, golfers who tend to swing over the top with a steep angle of attack can damage the inside ligaments and muscles of the back-side elbow (the right elbow in a right-handed golfer). This injury is the same as "Little Leaguer's elbow," a problem that many of us suffered with during our glory days as Little League stars. Joe Montana suffered the same injury and received corrective surgery for it during his last few years playing professional football. Hitting off mats—which simply cover the hard cement underneath it—can magnify the stress caused by an over-the-top swing plane, and can cause further damage to the elbow, hand, or wrist. The best way to prevent elbow injuries is to strengthen the forearms, shoulders, and wrists while practicing your grip and swing plane. Teeing up the ball when you hit off mats is a good idea too.

ROTATOR CUFF TENDINITIS OR STRAIN

The lead shoulder is perhaps the most important, yet least understood, body part in the golf swing. Recently, an injury to Greg Norman exemplified the importance of the left shoulder (in right-handed golfers) in the game of golf. Stress placed on his shoulder had caused his posterior capsule (the broad ligament that prevents the ball of humerus from sliding backward) to stretch and loosen over the years. This looseness in turn led to weakness of the rotator cuff muscles and tendons, and an inability to swing without pain. Ernie Els, Mark McCumber, Gil Morgan, and Dottie Pepper have all suffered from similar shoulder problems in recent years.

During the backswing, the arm is taken all the way across the body, potentially pinching off the soft-tissue structures on the front side of the shoulder joint (rotator cuff tendons and bursa). At the same time, the posterior muscles and ligaments of the shoulder and shoulder blade are stretched to their maximum length. These two positions commonly contribute to what is known as "rotator cuff impingement syndrome," in which the rotator cuff tendons and an adjacent bursa sac get pinched between the head of the humerus and the end of the clavicle. Although impingement syndrome is most common with baseball players and swimmers, it is also very common among golfers.

During the golf downswing, the lead arm must maintain the downswing plane, simultaneously resisting the dominating power of the right arm and shoulder. As this happens, the lead rotator cuff muscles must contract to rotate the arm to a square, neutral position and to stabilize the socket joint. The strain placed on the four small rotator cuff muscles of the shoulder is extremely high—and potentially damaging.

Tissue damage to the rotator cuffs can occur as a result of fatigue and overuse, from impingement syndrome, or from a strain in the muscle belly or tendon. Poor posture, poor shoulder mechanics, muscle imbalance in the shoulders, and poor shoulder flexibility are other possible causes of rotator cuff dysfunction.

The best way to prevent shoulder problems is to improve your posture and strengthen the rotator cuff muscles, while monitoring—and curtailing, if necessary—the number of balls you hit in practice. Chapter Six gives you several good exercises to strengthen your rotator cuff muscles.

AN EFFICIENT, LOW-INJURY GOLF SWING

In Chapter Six you learned exercises to improve your strength and flexibility, reduce your potential for injury, and improve your performance. Here we focus on swing biomechanics as they are influenced by limits of the body. To obtain a golf swing that is productive for you and limits your susceptibility to injury, you must understand the biomechanics of a typical swing and how the body reacts to this complex motion. This information will help you prevent injury and reduce physical stress on your body. It will also help you understand some of the factors associated with successful ballstriking. However, the intricate details of the full golf swing are not the focus of this chapter. The assistance of qualified and experienced PGA or LPGA teaching professionals should be sought for these purposes (refer to Chapter Three).

Try using the "Eight Commandments of Golf Performance" to structure your practice and play. The Eight Commandments are not strict rules. They are simple concepts you can follow to improve your level of performance with as little pain and frustration as possible. Incorporating the "Eight Commandments of Golf Performance" into your game may help you simplify your learning and practice by reducing anxiety and curtailing expectations.

Contrary to what you see when Ernie Els and Davis Love III swing a club, the golf swing is a very complex movement. When done successfully, it's a series of precise, coordinated, high-speed joint actions and muscle contractions. When each kinetic link (joint, muscle, etc.) works with the proper timing, speed, and energy, an efficient and reproducible swing is generated, in much the same way that the rowers of a crew move in perfect harmony, contributing equal speed, power, and timing, in helping the boat to run smoothly. But the very complexity of your swing means the chances for error and for your physical breakdown are high. Although a golfer may understand the physics of the golf swing, most don't realize that our bodies are not designed to produce such physics repeatedly.

Complicated machines such as computers work only well when all parts are working properly. Both the hardware and the software need to function properly for the computer to work. If the software is not designed properly, the computer's latest, greatest hardware technology won't perform to its potential.

Likewise with the golf swing. One misfiring link early in the swing, caused by fatigue, improper motion, or injury can drastically affect other links in the chain of events. Some top instructors believe that many swing errors are made within the first three feet of the

THE EIGHT COMMANDMENTS OF GOLF PERFORMANCE BY PAUL R. GEISLER, MA, ATC/L

1. *The full golf swing is* not *a natural motion for the human body.*

2. *The full golf swing is the most physically complicated motion of any sport.*

3. *The golf swing involves keeping both feet on the ground for most of the motion and is thus a* closed-chain *event. Closed-chain events are more mechanically complex and dynamic, and thus present more opportunities for the human body to compensate and break down.*

4. *The golf swing is a* closed skill, *which means that it requires the golfer to self-pace his play. This places psychological demands on golfers that are greater than those of other sports.*

5. *The constant elements involved in hitting a good golf shot are the club* path *and* face. *Skilled golfers can reproduce the proper path and square the face at the proper time, regardless of the quality and/or complexity of the motion required.*

6. *The only thing that can interfere with a golfer's path is the golfer's* body. *The more the body gets in the way, the more complicated the swing becomes. As the swing becomes more complicated, more practice is required to ensure reproducibility; higher levels of stress on the body are produced, which causes more injury; and higher levels of physical talent and mental toughness are required to sustain the swing under pressure.*

7. *All players fall into one of two categories with respect to biomechanics:*

    a. *Those with biomechanically sound golf swings that produce successful results with minimal maintenance. These players require less swing tuning and tweaking and have lower injury rates over time. Ray Floyd, Tom Lehman, Jeff Maggert, Bruce Lietzke, and Kelly Robbins are examples.*

    b. *Those with biomechanically complicated golf swings that require high skill levels to reproduce, and result in significantly higher levels of physical stress and injury. These players have to practice constantly and stay fit to maintain their level of play and physical health. Fred Couples, Tom Kite, Lee Trevino, and Nancy Lopez are examples.*

8. *Everyone has an ideal golf swing. It is difficult to duplicate the swing of any one player on professional tours. Trying to do so will result in frustration and possibly injury. The player must then constantly revamp the swing, undergo cyclical periods of improvement and regression, and perhaps sustain injury or suffer higher levels of pain.*

backswing, and that the rest of the swing becomes merely a series of compensations to correct the initial error. A weak link in your swing can cause a bad shot or cause you to make compensations in the swing to produce a good shot. Either scenario leads to inconsistent performance and a higher chance of injury.

A left-knee injury, for example, can disrupt the timing of the downswing and drastically influence the outcome of a shot. The player may unknowingly change his swing to improve the outcome of the shot, and compensating for the weak link only makes matters worse. The weak link also leads to higher levels of physical stress on the body. Many golf injuries start this way, eventually blossoming into physical disabilities that require medical attention. Identifying the weak link is the first and most important step in making the proper adjustment.

Improper trunk motion during the setup and backswing may also lead to compensation in a swing. A golfer may use his arms and hands, the last links in the chain, to try to "save" the shot. Compensating in this way is like a builder compromising on the integrity or structure of a house's foundation. You can guess what happens down the road after the roof has been put on and the house is occupied.

A similar compensation phenomenon is often seen in baseball. Many pitchers' elbow and shoulder injuries are actually rooted in poor biomechanics involving the larger, base segments of the body, like the legs and trunk. An early error (like losing balance during the windup) may cause the pitcher to make compensations with his pitching arm in order to throw a strike.

Let's discuss some basic drills designed to help you avoid injuries caused by an improperly sequenced swing motion, or what sports medicine professionals call a "kinetic chain."

A HEALTHY SETUP AND ADDRESS POSITION

A setup position, the first link in a golfer's kinetic chain, should look like that in Figure 7.1. The back should be straight with a vertical alignment of the shoulders, arms, kneecaps, and feet. This primary spinal angle promotes maximum anatomical rotation and stability of the spine. It also helps maintain your center of gravity, which optimizes balance and helps set the stage for a proper backswing path. A proper backswing can occur when the body does not impede the arms and club as they move into the backswing. The correct primary spinal angle, often referred to as the "athletic ready position," also creates a natural-looking angle at the hip and torso, called a "hip hinge." A proper hip hinge provides a relaxed and proper flexion angle in the knee joints. This is the only position in which the body is statically and dynamically balanced—that is, while at rest and in motion. A correct hip hinge is an important attribute of all fine motor athletic movements.

FIGURE 7.1

Example of good primary spine angle. Notice that the back is straight, with a vertical alignment of the shoulders, arms, kneecaps, and feet.

Many golfers lose this position by bending their spine into a curve during the setup, as seen in Figure 7.2. This position is easy to fall into, because it is the posture that many people assume when seated for prolonged periods. Gravity also contributes to an inefficient posture, which can lead to lower-back pain and discomfort. In addition, many golfers automatically position themselves in a way that feels natural but is not necessarily functional.

A slouched posture, called "spinal flexion," makes the golf swing less efficient. Spinal flexion causes problems for many golfers, including placing the golfer's body weight on his heels; decreasing the spine's ability to rotate by 20 to 50 percent; placing higher stress on the spine; and interfering with the backswing path.

The last problem usually occurs this way: The slouched posture places the hands closer to the body, causing the legs to interfere with the hands at the start of the backswing. Consequently, the golfer is forced to either manipulate the hand position at setup (pushing the hands out toward the ball) or reroute the backswing path in an

FIGURE 7.2

Example of poor primary spine angle. Notice the bending of the player's back and the curve in the spine during setup. This limits the ability to rotate fully.

attempt to keep the club on plane. Both compensations are inefficient and complicate the entire swing.

The first step in optimizing your golf swing is to evaluate the two
key kinetic links in the swing: the primary spine angle and the secondary spine angles. Once these two links are correct, you can work on
the rest of your swing more effectively and dynamically with the help of
your PGA or LPGA teaching professional. (You can achieve a proper primary spine angle by doing the hip-hinge drill. See page 86.)

THE IMPORTANCE OF THE SECONDARY SPINE ANGLE

The secondary spine angle is the angle of your spine that results from
the right hand being lower than the left in the grip of a right-handed
golfer (see Figures 7.3a and 7.3b). Most golfers naturally achieve this
spine angle at setup, but golf instructors say that a player must maintain this angle during the backswing to avoid a reverse pivot. There
are two reasons for this: Mechanically, maintaining the secondary
spine angle allows for a natural swing path during both the backswing
and downswing, with minimal compensations. Any change of angle
during the backswing causes a lateral shift during the downswing as
the body tries to reestablish the original spine and club positions.

Anatomically, a correct secondary spine angle improves free
rotation and decreases the stress placed on the spine. Amateur
golfers generate between 50 and 80 percent greater spinal loads than
professionals do, which requires 50 percent greater activity of the
trunk muscles and produces a swing with 34 percent less clubhead
speed than that of the pros (Hosea et al., 1990). Professional golfers
generally do a much better job of maintaining the secondary spine
angle throughout the swing, whereas many amateurs do a combination of reverse-pivot and lateral slide motion. This should be a concern of all players and teachers.

EXERCISE FOR IMPROVING SECONDARY SPINE ANGLE
This drill (see Figures 7.4a and 7.4b) will help to solidify your secondary spine angle, and simplify your golf swing. Perform this drill a

FIGURE 7.3a

Proper secondary spine angle at address

FIGURE 7.3b

Proper secondary spine angle at the top of the swing

FIGURE 7.4a

Drill to improve secondary spine angle

FIGURE 7.4b

Drill to improve secondary spine angle

minimum of 10–15 minutes every day until you can do it with a club in your hand and then with a ball in front of you.

1. Stand in a proper hip hinge with a club held across your chest, as shown. Stand in front of a mirror to watch your motion and angles.

2. Lower your right shoulder as you would when gripping the club in your hands. Be careful not to open your shoulders as you do this; remain square to the target line.

3. Align your head with your torso so that your chin bisects your chest in a parallel fashion.

4. Keeping your legs and hips still, slowly rotate your shoulders to the right so that your left shoulder replaces your right. Be sure to keep your head still, and be careful not to drop your left shoulder toward the ground.

5. Rotate on a plane so that if you shot a bullet out of the butt end of the club, it would hit you in the chest (in the mirror). Don't let it hit you in the hips or legs, as this will cause you to lose your spine angle.

6. Be sure to stop rotating when your body "wants to," and don't overrotate. Signs of overrotating are losing your spine angle and/or losing your initial rear-knee angle. Watch your motion in the mirror; don't look down to check yourself.

7. When you can do this, gradually add speed to mimic the true speed of your backswing. Slow down if your motion begins to become poor—quality is more important than speed. As you improve, do the drill with your eyes closed.

8. Perform the same drill with the downswing and finish position from the backswing position, keeping your shoulders and hips the same horizontal level throughout.

Improving the primary and secondary spine angles may seem like a simplistic approach to improving your golf game and decreasing injuries, but it is the best place to start. It is just as important as making sure that the foundation of your new home is solid, square, and of the proper dimensions. As mentioned earlier, the shoulders, arms, and hands react to the preceding actions of the torso, hips, and legs. Therefore, if improper rotation and loss of spine angle are corrected, the physical stress on the spine and upper extremities is lessened and so is the chance of injury. In short, improving spine angles produces a simple, efficient, and reproducible golf swing.

FINAL THOUGHTS

It is beyond the scope of this book to detail all golf injuries, their mechanism, and their treatment and prevention. This chapter is an attempt to address the most common injuries and their relation to swing mechanics. As is true of all sports, some golf injuries are the result of preexisting physical weaknesses that become manifest following a specific activity. Some injuries are due simply to the nature of the sport and exemplify the axiom "if you play something long enough, you will get hurt." Therefore, you should combine proper conditioning and training techniques with an approach to the golf swing that is biomechanically sound and fits your body's specific anatomical makeup.

CHAPTER EIGHT

EAT YOUR WAY
TO LOWER SCORES

*Picture yourself driving down the highway on the way to
the golf course. You read a billboard touting a product that
claims to reduce your risk of heart disease, block the development of cancer, keep off unwanted pounds, and shave
strokes off your golf game. . . . All for just pennies a day!*

Wouldn't you want to try it? Well, such a powerful tool is within
your grasp. With minimal planning and a little creativity, a
diet can reduce your risk of serious illness and improve your daily
golf performance. Most Americans will try any diet in an effort to
improve performance, stay healthy, or lose weight. Often, however,
the search for that elusive "magic potion" ends in a person's becoming a victim of "nutrition fraud" (buying a nutrition product that
cannot support its claims) and a complete disregard of sound nutrition practices.

Success on the golf course, as in any other endeavor in life,
requires commitment to basic practices and beliefs. A person's level
of motivation in honoring these practices and beliefs is key to
improving athletic performance. In no area is this more true than
one's eating habits. Altering your diet for a month to lose a few
pounds or increase your stamina is not enough to produce permanent changes in your game. To get long-lasting benefits from eating

healthfully, a person has to change his lifestyle until a new routine is established or the health-related goal is attained.

In the world of sports, nutrition is a hot topic and is finally receiving the attention of researchers and players. Nutritionists today know how to augment an athlete's endurance and strength and improve an athlete's focus and concentration. Nutrition has become a concern of both elite and recreational athletes, especially since the latter are prone to more stress, sweat more profusely, and use more carbohydrate as fuel. Less trained athletes also break down more protein and recover more slowly from exhaustion.

Until recently golf has been classified as a nonphysical sport, giving golfers an excuse to ignore advice about diet in athletics. But, whether you play as a career or a hobby, you know that golf is both physically and mentally demanding. Skill, coordination, and practice are essential if you want to shoot low scores. And golfers also must be able to adapt to intense heat and long hours. Heat can take its toll by dehydrating a golfer, and long hours on the practice tee and golf course can sap energy stores.

So what is the essence of eating to compete? It's finding the best program of nutrition for you and sticking to a few sound nutritional guidelines. To be effective, a program of nutrition should include a well-balanced training diet as well as a competition diet. There is no single recommendation for everyone. A diet should be based on an individual's fitness level and food preferences. A solid nutrition plan and training diet does not permit food fads, risky diets, or unproven formulas. It must include a daily commitment to maintaining ideal weight, eating a variety of foods, and strategic meal timing. Your peak performance diet should have menus designed to meet the caloric and nutrient demands of other sports and workout routines, and should address issues such as hydration, pregame meals, and powerful snacks.

THE SIX BASIC NUTRIENTS

Carbohydrates, fats, proteins, vitamins, minerals, and water are the six classes of nutrients that support the human body. They meet three basic needs of the body: to provide energy, to support new-tissue growth and tissue repair, and to regulate metabolism.

Carbohydrates are the main source of fuel for your muscles. "Carbs" come from the sugars and starches in foods you consume every day. A high-carbohydrate diet is necessary to maintain muscle glycogen—the primary fuel for most athletes—so a high-carbohydrate meal is considered by many to be the meal of champions. To keep your muscles energized and your mind alert, you should get 60–70 percent of your calories from quality-carbohydrate foods—foods high in complex carbohydrates, such as rice, breads, pasta, vegetables, fruits, fruit juices, cereals, and grains. These foods supply more protein, fiber, vitamins, and minerals as compared to foods rich in poor-quality carbohydrates. These are foods that are processed or contain high amounts of simple sugar, such as cakes, candies, and table sugar.

The body uses fats as a stored energy source. Most Americans now realize that saturated fat and high-cholesterol foods are linked to heart disease and cancer, and that fats from vegetable oils and fish offer many health benefits. Up to 25 percent of your daily calories can come from unsaturated fats. Small amounts of these healthy fats can also help you control hunger.

Protein, a component of all body tissues, is necessary for repairing and rebuilding muscles that break down during physical activity, for making hormones and enzymes, and for the transport of other nutrients. Protein comes from both animal and plant sources: from fish, chicken, veal, lamb, other meats, and eggs, and from soy, beans, legumes, and nuts. Protein does have calories, but it is used for energy only if you run out of carbohydrates. Most nutritionists agree that athletes in both strength and endurance sports need protein intake sufficient to cover loss of muscle protein and hormones.

Vitamins and minerals are the metabolic regulators needed to gauge chemical reactions in the body. Contrary to popular belief, these substances do not provide calories or energy. The delicate balance of foods and vitamin and mineral content determines our overall health and performance status.

Fifty-five percent of your weight is water, which is often called the most essential of all the nutrients. Dehydration, or loss of body water, can impair performance and increase the risk of heat illness.

KEEP YOUR EATING IN PLAY

Most athletes engage in daily training, but many are less committed to a daily food regimen. A busy lifestyle can rob someone of the time needed to select the most nutritious foods and prepare good meals. In our country, reliance on fast food, convenience foods, and products that promise the optimal diet in a glass, often sabotages even the best intentions. These foods are ineffective for a daily training diet and for precompetition meals. Avoid the hype and stick to the following basics:

Start the Day Right

If you are ever out on the course at 7:00 A.M. you may feel you have a good excuse for not eating a good breakfast. However, the cost of missing that morning meal is high. Refueling your muscles with readily available energy is essential if you want to achieve consistently excellent athletic performance, whether in a practice round or competition. Most golfers do get a bite of food in before the first tee, but often the meal is limited to something like a donut and a cup of coffee.

When time is not on your side, the following suggestion may be helpful: Get 60 percent or more of your calories from carbohydrates with a protein complement, which will help to keep your energy level high all day. Try one of these carbohydrate-rich meals:

- cereal, banana, orange juice, low-fat milk
- muffins or bagels with jam, yogurt, or dried fruit
- pancakes, French toast, or waffles with syrup; juice; milk
- pita bread with one or two slices of low-fat cheese; fruit; and juice

Mix It Up

Eat a variety of foods. Foods vary in their amounts of vitamins, minerals, proteins, and fiber. Some food, like meats and fish, are high in protein. Other foods provide a lot of vitamins, such as the vitamin C found in citrus fruits. A food such as bran is a good source of fiber.

To balance your daily intake of carbohydrates, proteins, fats, minerals, and vitamins, eat foods from the five food groups: bread and grains, fruit, vegetable, meat and fish, and dairy. Your ability to recover and refocus is limited when you eat a single food or from a single food group. In other words, eat healthful snacks and lunches—meals that provide the six basic nutrients. Your body will appreciate it.

Food for Thought

Most golfers take four hours to play a round, and longer if play is slow. That is why endurance is a factor in golf—the endurance to maintain concentration and focus at peak efficiency. A loss of energy and focus can happen at any time during a round, but it usually occurs after one and a half to two hours of play, depending on what was eaten for breakfast.

Those who participate in aerobic sports are forced to address the food issue for fear of "hitting the wall"—a phrase used to describe when a person suddenly feels a drop in energy, headache, light-headedness, or muscle pain during exercise. It's a signal from the body that its fluid or nutrient needs are being taxed. Golf is a slower game than other sports, with less dramatic signals from the body, but the results can be the same—less resistance to distraction, weakness, irritability, and loss of fluidity, to mention a few. These are the same symptoms seen with a drop in blood sugar and inadequate protein/calorie intake.

These problems can be easily prevented with adequate—and correct—fluid and food intake prior to the round. Even if you grabbed a glass of juice and a bagel, you're not protected. Both of these foods are composed primarily of carbohydrates, which give you immediate energy but are digested rapidly, resulting in little stamina for the back nine. Fat and protein are digested at a much slower rate; a protein source such as peanut butter, almonds, skim milk, or a hard-boiled egg can give you a feeling of fullness and hence more "staying power." A light snack of a fruit bar and some nuts on the ninth hole will improve your focus to the finish. If you are too hot to eat crackers or pretzels, try a cool carbohydrate source like fruits and vegetables with high water content—plums or orange sections, for example.

A helpful hint: Fill an ice-cube tray with juice and freeze. Before playing a round, place these frozen juice gems in a small cooler or insulated bag and toss them in your golf bag. You will appreciate not only their cooling power but also the vitamins, nutrients, and calories they provide. Chilled cucumber slices, cherry tomatoes, and celery sticks can also help you hydrate and energize at the same time.

Meal replacements such as Power Bars and Balance Bars are a convenient combination of carbohydrates and protein. Liquid alternatives such as Boost, Gator Pro, and Slimfast also contain a balance of nutrients that give you replacement energy. Try different brands or flavors to find the best one for you.

THE REALITY OF FAT

Even though fat makes a significant contribution to your staying power during endurance sports, increasing your intake of dietary fats is usually not necessary. Americans average 37 percent of calories from fat, far above the recommended minimum of 30 percent. Approximately one-third of adult Americans are overweight, and the number is rising. If you plan to eat more carbohydrates and protein-rich foods, it's best to try to cut fat wherever possible. Check for the hidden fats in dairy products, meat, eggs, nuts, and fried foods. Baked goods, chips, and fast food also serve up plenty of fat grams.

Suggestions for cutting the fat: Put jam on bread instead of butter. Use low-fat spreads such as mustard on sandwiches instead of mayonnaise or oil. Use low-fat bean dips on crackers instead of cheese. And choose your meats carefully. Tuna and other kinds of fish are an excellent source of protein and are low in saturated fats. Lean cuts of beef, chicken, and turkey will provide you with protein without any extra fat. Prime rib, pepperoni, sausage, and bacon have much higher fat contents. Angel food cake, fresh raspberries with Cool Whip, and fruit cobbler are ways to have your cake and eat it too. Baked chips and pretzels are healthy alternatives to potato chips.

HYDRATION BEFORE YOU REACH THE 19TH HOLE

When I watch long-distance runners train on Sunday afternoons, or take in a recreational tennis match, I commonly see the participants stop at regular intervals to rehydrate. In golf this is less common, but it shouldn't be. Constant hydration can improve your stamina and prevent fatigue on the golf course. Decreases in blood volume and cellular dehydration can occur when fluid is lost during exercise done in hot, humid conditions. Dehydration contributes to fatigue and increases the risk of cramping and headache. You must pay attention to your body and the signals it gives you. As the moisture in the air increases, for example, it's harder for your body to cool down. If the air is saturated with water, less evaporation occurs even at cooler temperatures, and your body heat can build up. Consequently, you are not getting the cooling benefit of perspiration.

Athletes typically need between two and three quarts of fluid daily, since exercise greatly increases fluid requirements. *But don't wait until you are thirsty before consuming fluids!* Prepare for your round by drinking 8 to 16 ounces of fluid (water or a sports drink) 15 minutes before. This will lower your body's core temperature and reduce the stress heat places on your cardiovascular system. During play, drinking four ounces every 30 minutes is usually adequate.

Now let's look inside your water bottle. Sport drinks such as Gatorade contain sodium and carbohydrate, which are absorbed very quickly by the body and assist your working muscles. Diluted fruit juices also provide a carbohydrate boost. And, of course, water is always a good choice.

When it comes to drinks that contain alcohol or caffeine, an athlete needs to be especially careful. Drinking too much alcohol the night before a match will almost certainly affect your performance the next day. Alcohol is a diuretic, which means it causes increased water loss and makes rehydration harder. This dehydrating effect can impair your performance and increase the risk of heat-related fatigue and weakness. A central nervous system depressant, alcohol also reduces gross motor skills such as balance and coordination.

The use of caffeine to enhance athletic performance is a topic still under debate. Some studies suggest that caffeine enhances endurance during aerobic exercise. A long-distance runner may benefit from caffeine, because it helps to metabolize fats into energy during exercise. Caffeine also works as a brain stimulant, often making the athlete perceive that he is not working as hard.

People respond differently to the effects of caffeine. Some people think it picks them up before exercise. Other people become jittery and hyper. As a golfer, you should limit your consumption of coffee, tea, chocolate, and soft drinks with caffeine, especially before and during competition. If you get butterflies before playing or become anxious on the course, caffeine will only worsen the problem. Another characteristic of caffeine is that it has a diuretic effect—it actually makes you lose fluids faster during physical activity. If you play in hot weather, caffeine may increase your loss of fluids, which can lead to dehydration. Of course, this can have a negative effect on your performance.

Round Recovery

A recovery period is needed after any athletic activity. If you play back-to-back rounds, you need to awaken refreshed, alert, and well rested on the second day. This means that you have to pay particular attention to your recovery period following the first round. How well you recover depends on your food and beverage intake before, during, and after your activity. When you exercise for three hours or more, the nutrient composition of your diet during recovery is as important as what you consumed days before the event. Eating before you feel tired or hungry within 60 minutes of play, checking your fluids, and avoiding alcohol and caffeine are essential in bringing your body back to a point where it can produce a solid performance. What you eat after today's round is actually your pre-event meal for tomorrow.

FIND YOUR PERSONAL RHYTHM

Power, timing, consistency, and concentration are all elements of winning golf. The consistency of the pro holds the amateur in awe. Swing after swing, pros make it look easy. But a smooth, consistent swing does not happen by chance. It takes hours of practice, instruction, and fitness training. This training must include long hours on the course and practice range, as well as cross-training exercise that develops strength and endurance.

Just as one low round does not make a great player, one healthy meal or snack does not provide a basis for consistent and enhanced performance. Only a sustained lifestyle of healthy food choices and well-timed meals and snacks will improve your endurance and consistency, give you a body that adapts to physical exertion, and buffer you from the effects of stress.

The foods you eat can also affect you psychologically. For example, many athletes are superstitious about their pre-round meal: they eat the same meal before every round they play. They believe this ritual helps them perform better, even if there is no scientific basis for the claim. There is nothing wrong with this belief. Anything that makes you feel more confident is a plus in sports. If you get confidence and comfort from eating a certain meal before you play, by all means do so.

Taking a casual approach to diet can cause inconsistent play and a loss of focus. If you seem to be working too hard to get the results you want, then something may be wrong with your diet. To focus your energy and powers of concentration, several steps can be taken:

1. Obtain reliable advice on your calorie and protein needs from a nutritionist who can perform an analysis of your

current eating patterns and recommend changes based on your individual needs and the specific demands of golf.

2. Monitor changes in your play and try to determine whether there is any link between the timing of your meals and the type of foods you eat.

3. If you feel that something is working in your favor, give it a repeat trial.

4. Allow your training diet to mimic your diet for competition. For example, have it include the following:
   - timed meals and snacks
   - a balance of protein and carbohydrate for strength and energy
   - healthful eating both on and off the golf course

FINAL THOUGHTS

The guidelines contained in this chapter contain no magic formula for success. They adhere to basic nutritional principles of variety and moderation. There is no single nutrition prescription for all athletes, no single food we should revere or eschew. Rather, a healthy eating plan that takes into account your likes and dislikes is presented in this chapter.

You are human, and human nature usually has its way. For example, many athletes reward themselves with unconstrained food choices following a major event or an outstanding performance. But if you have a choice between spending your time on your training regime or an episode of self-indulgent eating, choose the training: it will ultimately pay off in a more fit body that performs at peak levels. A Canadian physician, Sir William Osler, who died in 1919, eloquently summarized this principle:

There is a master word that makes a champion a winner. For a little one, the master word looms large indeed. It is the open sesame to every portal. The great equalizer in the world. True philosopher's stone which transmutes all the base metal of humanity into pure gold—the stupid it will make bright; the bright brilliant, and brilliant steady. To youth it brings hope and accomplishments, to the middle-aged, confidence, to the aged, repose. It is directly responsible for all the advancements in medicine and sports in the past 50 years. Not only has it been the touchstone of progress there, but also it is the measure of success in everyday life. And the master word is "WORK."

Success at golf doesn't just happen. It is the result of total training—your training from the dinner table to the tee. Quality nutrition can help set the tempo of a sound training program.

CHAPTER NINE

TOURNAMENT PREPARATION AND PLAYING STRATEGIC GOLF

John hits a tee shot into the trees. Instead of electing to chip out sideways and play for an up-and-down par, or at worse bogey, he tries to hit a fantasy shot over and around the trees in front of him. Although he never hits this type of shot in practice, he's too proud to chip out and "take his medicine." His ego gets in the way of decision making; he steps beyond the limits of his skills and plays a low-percentage recovery shot. He confidently plays the shot, but the ball strikes a tree and goes out of bounds. He has to replay from the same spot and take a penalty stroke. He chips the ball back into play, because he knows that making the shot is beyond his ability. He makes a triple bogey on the hole and is furious: he should have made no worse than a bogey, but his earlier decision to try for a fantasy shot ruined his performance on the hole.

This type of thinking was perpetuated in the movie *Tin Cup*, starring Kevin Costner. On the last hole of the U.S. Open, Costner, playing an egomaniacal golf pro, decides to go for a 250-yard carry over the water. He thinks he can make the shot and is confident when he steps up over the ball. But he dunks shot after shot into the water before finally holing out with the last ball in his bag.

Poor risk management is a killer of low scores. Conversely, an ability to manage risk and play smart usually results in good scores. The smart golfer devises a strategy for every round based on his skills, then implements the plan. Still, many golf teachers neglect course management skills and game plan development, even at the professional level.

One of the distinctive features of golf is that it is a thinker's game. A golfer who knows when and when not to take risks will always beat the golfer who is a prisoner to his ego and emotions. A reckless game plan coupled with overconfidence is a sure recipe for high scores. Confidence is a great asset in golf, but overconfidence can prevent you from playing smart golf. You must have confidence to hit any shot well, but that doesn't mean letting your boldness cause you to hit a low-percentage shot. The overbold player usually reaches into his golf bag to drop another ball into play. Pulling out a driver on every par 4, cutting the corner on every dogleg, going for every par 5 in two, and aiming at the pin on every hole may yield an occasional birdie but more often this approach leads to double bogeys.

On the other hand, a cautious or careful game plan will not necessarily help you score well either. A player may be so afraid of making errors that he becomes overcautious. This player is in "protect mode," which can lead to tentative swings and fearful putting. In protect mode, the goal is to avoid making a high number or a mistake, which is a tense way to play golf. Have you ever putted well when trying not to three-putt every green? Probably not.

Good course management and a sound game plan translates to smart golf. The smart golfer balances both conservative and bold shots at the right times, assessing the risk-reward ratio on every shot. What are the risks of going for a par 5 in two on a particular hole? What are the rewards? The rewards are simple—a possible birdie or maybe a chance at eagle. What are the risks? Scoring a double or triple bogey. When evaluating the risk-reward ratio of a decision, you should consider many factors. Is water or out-of-bounds in play? If you leave it short, are you still in good shape? What's over the green? Is the green receptive, and will it hold a shot? Is it an easy up and down, or would you be better off laying up and hitting a full shot into the green?

This chapter discusses three areas of course management: studying the course, making a game plan to play the course, and carrying out the game plan. Paying attention to the details of the course, picking smart targets off the tees, and becoming familiar with the contours of the greens are the keys to studying a course. This can be accomplished during a practice round or, if you can't play a practice round, by walking the golf course. The second part of course management is developing a game plan you can later put into action on the golf course. Lastly, it's important to stick to your plan but be flexible with the plan when necessary.

GETTING TO KNOW THE COURSE

A practice round should be part of your tournament preparation, and it's the start of a good game plan. Most tour professionals play one or more practice rounds before a tournament starts. The better tour caddies walk the course backward before practice rounds to check distances in the yardage book, look for course changes, and determine the best approach shots. The best time to check the accuracy of the golf course's yardage book is during the practice round, not after you fly the green on an approach shot during the first round. If you are unfamiliar with the course, a practice round is also helpful in selecting good targets off the tees and determining distances for carrying fairway or greenside bunkers, which assists you with club selection during actual tournament rounds. If you pick smart targets during practice rounds, you won't be forced to focus on avoiding trouble areas during the tournament.

STUDY THE GREENS

A practice round should also be used to get to know the subtle breaks on the greens. A smart golfer devotes time to studying the greens before a tournament starts. Course knowledge and experience on the greens is key to reading the greens correctly. Does your local course knowledge help you to putt better? Yes, for sure! And if you're playing a new course, it's even more important to get to know the greens. Tour pros hit several putts on each green during practice rounds to familiarize—or refamiliarize—themselves with the greens. Many pros draw up diagrams of the breaks on each green for use during the tournament.

If you have the time, hit several putts from different locations on the green—uphill, downhill, and across the green. Watch the ball as it rolls and takes breaks in the green. This is especially vital on greens with two or three tiers. It's often hard to judge how a tier will affect your ball until you have hit a few putts on the green. Make sure you hit some putts from the top to the bottom tier, and vice versa.

Get to know the speed, slope, grain, and trouble areas of each green. Usually the grain grows downhill or toward the setting sun. Putts attempted downgrain will be much faster. Carefully watch each putt you hit and notice its speed and the direction of its slope. See how long it takes for each putt to slow down. Lock into your memory the image of each putt you hit so you have something to draw on in the tournament. In addition, note the places to leave your shot that will give you the best putts given the possible pin positions. For example, putts from above the pin on greens that are sloped from back to front are usually fast and tricky. Furthermore, note where the trouble areas or sucker pins may be located.

You can also ask the local head pro to tell you his experience with the greens. Ask which greens require that you stay below the hole. Ask if there are any greens on which a putt may be read to break one way but actually breaks the opposite way. Find out where you should not short-side yourself if you miss the green.

Check Distances to the Greens

Most courses have detailed yardage books. If the course you will be playing doesn't, measure the distances from the yardage plates or markers to the middle of the green and note any discrepancies you find. Even yardage books become outdated and give false distances, especially if some of the greens or tees have been redone. For this reason, a smart player will check the yardage book's accuracy every year during practice rounds.

Another of your pretournament tasks: record the distance from the tee box to fairway bunkers and the distance to carry fairway bunkers from the tee. This information will help with club selection off each tee. Note the distance to any other hazards adjacent to the fairway, such as water, and measure the distance to carry any bunkers that front the greens. Check the depth of each green so you can calculate the distance behind pins that are located on the rear portion of the green.

Don't forget to calculate the distance you have to hit a lay-up shot on par-5 holes. To do this, calculate the distance from the sprinkler head nearest to where your tee shot usually comes to rest to 20 yards short of the hazard. Many players just bash two shots on a par 5 to see how close they can get to the green. This is a bad idea if you can't control the yardage on shots from inside 100 yards. Often it's better to lay back to a distance you are more consistent from. Make sure you have a full swing for your third shot with your favorite wedge. This will allow you to better control the distance of your approach shot.

STUDY THE COURSE LAYOUT

Beyond studying the greens and checking distances, it's important to know the course layout so you can formulate a game plan for the tournament. The design and layout of each hole will influence the targets you select for tee shots and approach shots, and the clubs you select off the tees. If the hole is a dogleg that turns abruptly, your chances of hitting a tee shot through the fairway are greater. This may dictate that you hit an iron or fairway wood off the tee. A shorter hole with a narrow fairway gives you the option of hitting an iron or fairway wood off the tee. If the course has smaller greens that put a premium on hitting the green in regulation, this also dictates your target selection.

You should also study the landing area of each fairway. Some courses are designed with fairways that have a landing area wider than the rest of the fairway. Calculating the distances to the "fat" part of each fairway may increase your chance of hitting more fairways. Also consider the best angle to hit an approach shot when you select targets from the tees. If a green has a deep bunker fronting the left side, your best approach is from the right side of the fairway so you have a clear shot to the flag. The size of each green and the presence of any bunkers or water around the greens are also considerations in the game plan. I don't want players to play "avoidance golf"—steering clear of trouble areas around the green—but I do want them to know when to play to the middle part of the green. You should never focus on where *not* to hit your ball or the spot to leave a shot that would make a sure bogey, but this is vital information for planning shots and picking smart targets. Once you plan the shot and pick a target, the goal should be to focus on where you want to hit the ball.

GAME PLAN NOTES FOR PAR-3 HOLES

- For each hole in the practice round, record the clubs you hit, wind direction, and result.
- Pick out eye-catching targets beyond the green (i.e., the top of a tall tree) that you can use during the tournament. Record them in the yardage book or your notes.
- In the yardage book record the distance to carry greenside bunkers or hazards.
- Determine the best spots on the green to putt from, given the possible pin locations for the tournament. Is the green sloped from back to front? Note the direction of the slope, grain, and undulations.
- In the yardage book, record the green depth from front to back. Also diagram the slope of the green and possible pin placements.
- Note the distance to carry the ball to the top tier of any two-tiered green.
- Note the firmness of the green and amount of roll after landing on the green.

MAKE YOUR GAME PLAN

Now that you've studied the course and greens, checked accuracy of yardage markers, measured the distance to carry bunkers, and picked smart targets, it's time to develop a specific plan for playing the course. A game plan is a strategy you use to score your best on any course. Your philosophy about how to score your best guides the decisions you make on the course. A game plan comes from your knowledge of the course, your course management skills, and your golfing strengths and weaknesses. It should fit your style of play, ability level, and strengths. I like game plans that keep a player focused on the process—that is, on playing one shot at a time. Many players focus too much on score during the round. A process-focused game plan, on the other hand, helps you focus on playing each hole and each shot, one at a time, to the best of your ability.

In tournament play, under pressure, it's easy to make poor decisions, so it's a good idea to decide on a game plan before the round. I want players to make decisions about their game plan when the emotions of the moment are not a factor.

For example, what are the decisions you make when you go for a green in two? What is the minimum distance you can safely hit your 3-wood or a long iron when going for a par 5? In what situations will you go for the green? First, decide which par 5s you can possibly reach. Second, during the practice round decide when you are going for the green—say, if you can safely hit a 3-wood or less to within 10 yards of the green. Finally, stick to your decisions as best you can when you play in the tournament. You may need to be flexible, however. For example, the decisions you make in the practice round may take into account changes in weather conditions or course setup. Maybe a par 5 you reached in two in the practice round is now playing longer because of a strong head wind. You may elect to lay up instead of going for the green in two.

Play Within Your Ability

We hear the saying "play within yourself" often, but what does it really mean? It means playing shots that you can hit with no difficulty on the range. It means not stepping beyond your skill level and trying to hit a fantasy shot. Say you have 240 yards to carry the water on a par-5 shot. You have never hit your 3-wood that far in the air on the range or in a round, but you attempt to do so today, because you feel if you hit it perfectly, you can carry the water. In this example, you are stepping beyond your ability and playing a low-percentage shot.

A game plan should reflect your current ability. If you are not a strong driver of the ball, this dictates hitting off the tee with an iron or fairway wood instead of your driver. If you are not a long-ball hitter, you may need to lay up on the long par 5s. If you are erratic with iron play, the best plan for you may be to shoot for the center of the green on most holes unless you have a short iron or wedge into the green.

THE GOALS OF A GAME PLAN

A game plan for playing a course may be as simple as selecting one or two things you want to accomplish—for example, setting goals to hit 10 of 14 fairways and 13 of 18 greens for a round. The plan is then to hit as many fairways and greens as possible. I like this strategy, because it encourages you to focus on performing your best on each hole, which helps you score well without becoming preoccupied with your score.

Good results flow from accomplishing your process goals. But don't get carried away and make your goals too difficult or too numerous. If you have hit 10 greens on average for the last five rounds, for example, you don't want to set a goal of 15 greens.

Your game plan should also flow from your study of the course during the practice round. It may include notes you have made about what clubs you should hit on par-4 and par-5 holes. For example, if you have decided that hole number five is a three-shot par 5, you can plan to hit a 3-wood off the tee to increase your chances of hitting the fairway. You'll also want to consider when to hit an iron or 3-wood off the tee to stay short of a fairway bunker or to have a better chance of hitting the center of the fairway on a tight hole. In addition, your game plan may take into account the notes you have made of the clubs you hit off the par-3 holes, the direction of the wind, and results of the shot (pin high, short, or long). Any observation you have made during your practice-round study of the course gives you more information to help you plan your shots in tournament play.

I urge players to develop a strategy for approach shots. What clubs do you hit with the most confidence, and with which clubs do you feel you can aim at any flag? Wedge, 9-iron, 8-iron? Decide on the clubs that you'll use to take dead aim and which clubs you'll use to shoot at the center of the green. The size of each green influences your strategy here. If it's a smaller green, the high-percentage shot is to aim at the center of the green. Courses with small greens, like Harbour Town in Hilton Head, give you a legitimate chance at birdie on almost every hole if you hit the center of the green. When a pin is tucked close to a water hazard or a deep bunker, do you still take dead aim at the pin? Many of these decisions can be made before the start of a round, when emotions are less likely to push you to make rash decisions.

GAME PLAN NOTES FOR PAR-4 HOLES

- For each hole in the practice round record the clubs you hit, wind direction, and result.
- Pick out one or two eye-catching targets in the fairway (a tall tree or the edge of a bunker) and note them in the yardage book.
- Record in the yardage book the distance to stay short of and to carry fairway bunkers or hazards.
- Record the distance to the corner of any doglegs.
- Note the distance to the fat part of the fairway.
- Note the firmness of the fairway and the amount of roll.
- Decide on a club to hit given wind direction and other factors.
- In the yardage book, record the distance to carry greenside bunkers or hazards.
- Note the direction of the slope, grain, and undulations. What's the best area to putt from given the pin position? Is the green sloped from back to front?

- In the yardage book, record the green depth from front to back.
- Note the distance to carry the ball to the top tier of any two-tiered greens.
- Note the firmness of the green and the amount of roll after landing on the green.

STICK TO THE GAME PLAN, BUT BE FLEXIBLE

Once you decide on how to play the course and have a game plan, it's show time. However, executing the plan is difficult for some players. Often, the pressure of tournament competition causes a golfer's brain to misfire. The game plan may get thrown away when emotions become elevated, frustrations dominate the player's mind, or overconfidence takes control of the player's game. For example, the frustration of an early bogey or double bogey may create the urge to press and "get it back" on the next holes, which may cause you to throw out the game plan and play more aggressively. You hit driver instead of 3-wood, cut the corners on par 4s, and fire at tucked flags with your 3-iron. Likewise, a player who starts well and is playing better than expected may become protective and play more conservatively than the game plan dictates. Or a player who has it going early, and feels confident, may decide to play more aggressively than normal.

All three situations can cause a player to abandon a game plan. It's better to force yourself to stay with your plan instead of playing more aggressively or protecting your score.

I believe you must be flexible, though. For example, I urge players to take advantage of a round in which everything is working. This may be the time to take dead aim more often, fire at the pin, and make as many birdies as possible. Often a good player who gets a few under par early or mid-round feels anxious and wants to protect his score. This is not the best approach to finishing off a good round.

Some players prefer to base their game plan on how they are hitting the ball that day. Steve Jones says his game plan changes with his ballstriking. If he is playing well and is focused, he might take more risks and fire at more pins. When Jones shot 26 under par to win the 1997 Phoenix Open, his game plan was to make the best opportunity for birdie on each hole. Even though he was playing well, he didn't just fire recklessly at every pin.

One reason your game plan should be flexible is that a course usually plays differently from the practice round to tournament day. The conditions of the course, changes in wind direction and various other weather conditions, firmness of the greens, and positions of the pins will most likely change before and during the tournament. In the practice round, you may have planned to hit 3-wood off the first tee to stay short of the fairway bunker. On tournament day, however, a stiff wind may be blowing in your face on the first tee. Now a driver may be the correct club to hit—under these conditions, a driver will stay short of the bunker and result in a shorter approach to the green.

GAME PLAN NOTES FOR PAR-5 HOLES

- For each hole in the practice round record the clubs you hit, wind direction, and result.
- Pick out one or two eye-catching targets in the fairway (a tall tree or the edge of a bunker) and note them in the yardage book.
- In the yardage book record distances to stay short of and to carry fairway bunkers or hazards.
- Record distances to the fat part of the fairways.
- Decide on a club to hit off the tee given the wind direction and other factors.
- Record lay-up distance from the yardage markers in the fairway.
- Decide whether the hole is a two- or three-shot hole. Make decisions about going for the green in two.
- In the yardage book record the distance to carry greenside bunkers or hazards.
- What's the best area to putt from given the pin position? Is the green sloped from back to front? Note the direction of the slope, grain, and undulations.

- In the yardage book record the green depth from front to back.
- Note the distance to carry the ball to the top tier of any two-tiered greens.
- Note the firmness of the green and the amount of roll after landing on the green.

SET GOALS FOR YOUR GAME PLAN

I urge players to set goals to help them stay focused on execution and to play in the now. All great performances flow from a present execution focus. In golf, such a focus requires that you think about only the shot you're faced with right now. You can't make a birdie standing on the first tee, but you can get your ball into the fairway to give yourself a better chance of hitting the green and making birdie. To get the ball in the fairway, you have to focus on executing a good shot. This is why I like a game plan to include a specific number of fairways and greens that you decide on before the round.

I also recommend that a game plan have as many birdie opportunities as possible. You might define a birdie opportunity as a putt within 25 feet. If you are hitting 12 greens a round, and on half of the greens hit in regulation you are putting from 25 feet or less, then an appropriate goal is six birdie chances. This focuses you on making birdies and getting chances to make them. It doesn't mean you *have* to make them. The only way to score your best is to give yourself more chances at birdie. You can't make birdie if you miss the green on the short side of the flag.

As a sports psychologist, I usually have players include one or two mental goals in their game plans. Mental goals address the thought processes you need to improve. They may also be related to playing strategies you have been working on. A college golfer I worked with was losing his focus over the ball because he was erratic with his new preshot routine, which happens often when a player changes his routine. One goal we set for him was to stop and refocus for at least six shots during the round when he drifted this way. This became part of his game plan. Another example: if you find that you are getting lazy with selecting targets off the tee box, you may set a goal to pick a specific target in the fairway on every shot. This focuses you on playing process golf and approaching your game one hole at a time.

The following are other examples of mental goals:

- Visualize every shot before I step up to the ball.
- Be totally committed to the line I select for each putt.
- Stay focused on playing one shot at a time.
- Stay patient with my putting after I miss a putt.
- Be more accepting of myself after I hit a bad shot.
- Forget about bad shots within 10 seconds—don't dwell on them.
- Relax between shots and enjoy the day.

FINAL THOUGHTS

Use the following list when you are playing a practice round and formulating a game plan. You should bring a notebook or the course's yardage book with you so you can take notes for review later and for devising your game plan.

STUDYING THE COURSE

- check the accuracy of the yardage book or yardage plates
- measure distances to fairway bunkers and to carry greenside bunkers
- note the distance to the fat part of fairways
- pick smart targets off the tees
- study the contour, speed, and slope of the greens
- note trouble areas around the greens and diagram the slope of unfamiliar greens
- find the pin location on each green that will give you the best birdie chance

TEE SHOT CLUB SELECTION FACTORS

- length of hole
- tight or wide fairway
- wind direction
- trouble areas, such as bunkers, water, or out-of-bounds
- distance to hit through the fairway dogleg
- distance to the fat part of fairways
- confidence in driver and 3-wood

SOME GAME PLAN GOALS

- statistics that focus on the process (fairways hit, greens hit, up-and-down percentage, etc.)
- number of birdie opportunities
- keeping ball in play for 18 holes
- number of birdies
- number of one-putts/total feet of one-putts made
- goals to focus on routine (focus on the process, focus on visualizing shot, trust my swing)
- picking a specific target on every shot
- playing smart shots for 18 holes

CHAPTER TEN

THE FINAL PREP
FOR WINNING GOLF

A professional golfer would never plan to arrive at the course 10 minutes before his tee time, hit a few hurried shots on the range, and then rush to the first tee. This is not a good warm-up for golf. And some players are guilty of not warming up at all.

To play your best, you will want to prepare your best. If you neglect a preround warm-up, the first few holes become your driving range and practice green. A poor start to a round—say, a bogey or two—can give you a bad attitude for the entire round. To play your best golf right from the start, it's important to take time to prepare your body and mind to play. In this chapter you'll learn the keys to warming up before a round so you feel confident and ready to play your best. I also give you a one-hour precompetition warm-up routine. This routine covers everything you need to get ready— from stretching to getting focused—to play your best golf.

Keep in mind that a precompetition warm-up is not intended to be a practice. You use a warm-up for four purposes: to get loose and physically warm up, to focus the mind, to gain confidence, and to get a feel for your swing and tune up your touch on the greens.

Since the goal of practice is to make your swing and putting better, a practice mind-set is much different from the mentality you need for a warm-up. You practice to improve and prepare your game. You warm up to get ready to play your best and to get focused on your game—to leave the office, school, or business meetings behind you. The warm-up is not the time to work on your golf swing, try new equipment, or call your broker on the cell phone.

How do other athletes, such as sprinters, get ready for competition? They stretch and do preset warm-ups. But the sprinter is doing more than just getting loose. Besides loosening his muscles during a warm-up, he is making a transition from other areas of his life into his sport—in other words, getting on his "game face." He may also be visualizing the race and focusing on a plan for getting a good start.

As a golfer, you too should have a specific warm-up routine. Your warm-up is the time to loosen up and feel your swing that day. It's also when you should get focused on the opening holes, review your game plan, and hone your touch so you can play your best right out of the gate.

KEYS TO A FULL-GAME WARM-UP

The time needed to properly warm up before a round depends on the golfer's objectives and personal preferences. Most professionals spend an hour to an hour and a half warming up before a round. If you don't have an hour for a warm-up, try to set aside at least a half hour. The key is to have a routine—*any* routine—before you play.

The warm-up is a great time to make the switch from other activities in your life to golf. This does not mean you have to hit 200 balls and putt for an hour. In fact, I encourage you not to do so. The purpose of a warm-up is simply to feel confident, focused, and ready to play before you go to the first tee.

TAKE ENOUGH TIME

Leave home to arrive at the golf course with plenty of time to warm up. The worst habit players have is rushing the warm-up to make a 9:00 A.M. tee time. If you arrive at the course 35 minutes ahead of time, adjust your routine accordingly. If you arrive late and have only 20 minutes to warm up, don't panic and rush your warm-up. You don't want to feel rushed when you get to the first tee. This leads only to a racing mind and hurried swings.

Stretch Your Muscles

To loosen your muscles and avoid injury, stretch before you take any swings. Stretch the muscles in your shoulders, neck, back, and legs. As part of their routine, many tour pros stretch with the on-site fitness staff before every round. You should and can easily do a few basic stretches on your own, without the aid of a professional. For example, as part of his warm-up routine, Mark O'Meara swings two heavy clubs before hitting any balls to loosen the muscles in his shoulder and back.

The following is a three-minute stretching routine.

WARM-UP EXERCISES

This stretching program can be used prior to any practice session or tournament round. Hold each position for 4–6 seconds and repeat each exercise three times.

1. Back and hamstring stretch: Keeping your legs straight and your feet wider than shoulder width, hold a club in your hands (see Figure 10.1). Bend over from the waist and slowly lower your hands and the club to the ground in the middle of your stance. Be sure to keep your back straight and hinge at the hips. Don't bow your back. You don't need to touch the ground to be stretching the hamstrings in the back of your legs.

2. Chest and shoulder stretch: Holding a club in both hands at the ends, slowly raise your arms up (keeping both straight), over, and behind your head (see Figure 10.2). Keep your elbows straight and do not arch your back. Take the club as far as you can and stretch the front of your chest and shoulders.

3. Forearm stretch: Hold a club shaft in your hands with your palms down straight in front of you (see Figure 10.3). Keep your elbows straight and raise your arms to shoulder height. Slowly force your hands to the ground, stretching the tops of your forearms.

FIGURE 10.1

Back stretch

FIGURE 10.2

Chest and shoulder stretch

FIGURE 10.3

Forearm stretch

Reverse your hands and repeat the motion, stretching the insides of your forearms.

4. Left shoulder stretch: Hold a club with your left hand facing upward and your right hand facing downward, appoximately shoulder width apart (see Figure 10.4). Cross your left arm over your right toward your backswing, keeping your right elbow straight. Gradually push up and back with your right hand with the bottom part of the club, stretching your left shoulder. Repeat. Caution: if you have shoulder problems with your lead shoulder, be very careful with this stretch. If soreness increases during or after this stretch, discontinue it immediately.

5. Wrist stretch: Hold a pitching wedge in your right hand, using a proper golf grip and with your arm raised to shoulder height (see Figures 10.5a and 10.5b). Slowly lower and raise the club by hinging your wrists. Be sure to keep control of the club, and do not bend your elbow. Repeat with your left hand. Perform 15–20 repetitions with each hand.

FIGURE 10.4

Left shoulder stretch

FIGURE 10.5a

Wrist stretch

FIGURE 10.5b

Wrist stretch

6. Back and hips stretch: Take your stance and rotate to the backswing side, using the club as a lever behind your waist (see Figure 10.6). Use your front elbow to help push you. Remember to imitate your actual swing and stretch in both directions. Hold the stretch position for six seconds, repeat three times, and then move slowly into and out of this position continuously and with control. Do not bounce vigorously. Repeat for both sides.

7. Warm-up: Gradually warm up by swinging two clubs at once. Start with half swings at half speed and progress to full swings at half speed. When you start hitting shots, hit 10 half shots at half speed. Work up to full shots and build up to full speed.

START WITH A WEDGE

After you have stretched, take a sand wedge or pitching wedge and hit half shots to loosen up. Start with 10 half-speed and half-swing

FIGURE 10.6

Hip stretch. Imitate your actual swing as you stretch in both the backswing and forward swing directions.

shots. Then work up to a full swing with full speed. This gradual approach minimizes force on the joints and muscles and decreases the chance of injury. Don't hit the driver until you are warm and loose.

Work through the bag systematically. Many tour pros have a system of hitting the same clubs in the warm-up, usually odd irons or even irons. For example, you might use a wedge, 9-, 7-, 5-, and 3-iron. Then hit a couple of 3-woods and a few drivers. Don't forget to hit some specialty shots, such as knockdown shots or curving shots. Avoid hitting too many balls during warm-up. You want to loosen up, not wear yourself out. Pros typically hit only 30 to 40 shots, using six to eight clubs.

Finish your warm-up with a sand wedge. It's a good idea to finish with some smooth-tempo half shots. You never want to smash drivers just before you walk to the first tee. Ending the warm-up with a driver may increase your tempo and make you want to swing harder on the golf course.

REMEMBER THE GOALS OF THE WARM-UP

The purpose of the warm-up is not to practice your golf swing but to hit shots you will be required to hit on the course. Save work on your swing mechanics for your practice after the round. Now is the time to develop confidence in shots so that you can trust them on the course.

First, focus on hitting the ball solid—in the center of the club-face. Don't worry about hitting to a specific target yet. Second, swing in balance with good tempo. Preround swings should focus on ingraining a tempo and good balance. Don't worry if you hit some bad shots on the range; you will not necessarily hit those same shots on the course. Feel the good shots you hit.

SELECT ONE SWING CUE FOR THE ROUND

Many players I work with have a list of swing cues they have used when playing well. A swing cue is a thought or image that is used as a trigger to start the golf swing, such as a feeling of good balance or tempo. Many players ask me if it's good to have a swing cue. I answer that it's OK as long as the cue is not mechanical—such as the position of the club during the backswing—or swing-path-oriented. It's a good idea to pick a swing cue that's working on the range or that has worked well in past rounds.

Good swing cues come from tempo, feel, or balance. When you decide on a swing cue, link it to a feeling of what you want to accomplish with the swing. Stay away from giving yourself verbal instructions during your swing, such as "Keep the club parallel at the top." Instead, feel the result you want and use that as the swing cue. Once you have selected a swing cue, stick with it for the entire round.

Your swing cue doesn't have to be complex. You don't want to have a checklist of 15 different things to remember as you stand over the ball. This only clutters your mind.

FOCUS THE MIND

One purpose of your preround preparation is to focus the mind. This is the time to put on your game face, and to make the transition from other activities to golf.

SAMPLE ONE-HOUR WARM-UP ROUTINE

Arrive Early

Get to the course an hour and 10 minutes before your scheduled tee time. Check in with the pro shop or registration desk early.

Stretching (6 minutes)

Use a stretching routine to loosen up the body and prevent injury. Swing a couple of clubs to loosen up.

Full-Shot Warm-Up (19 minutes)

Hit half shots first, then work your way up to full shots. Use even or odd clubs, and work your way through your entire bag. Gain confidence in hitting solid shots, with a sound tempo. Don't worry about mechanics. Practice with the clubs that you will hit on the course.

Putting Warm-Up (10 minutes)

Hit some solid putts to control the roll of the ball. Generate a feel for the speed of the greens. Build confidence by making some putts from three feet or less. Use this time to click in your focus. Sharpen your preputt routine.

Short-Game Warm-Up (15 minutes)

Practice chipping and/or sand play. Get a feel for the conditions of the bunkers and rough. Use your visualization skills here—no mechanics. Observe the firmness of the green and how the ball reacts when it hits the green. Test how the ball comes out of the rough.

Relax (10 minutes)

Use the last 10 minutes or so to relax while getting to the tee in plenty of time. Make a final check of your equipment and go over your game plan for the first hole. Visualize what you need to do. Think about why you will play well today.

How should you get ready the last few minutes before you play? My advice is to hit shots with the same focus and intensity as when you play. Play actual shots; don't practice your swing. Don't just beat balls; instead, you should have a specific purpose for every shot. I recommend that you hit the last 10 shots with the full preshot routine that you use on the course.

Many players imagine playing the first few holes of the course on the range, which is a great way to get focused. Define boundaries in the range to help you imagine the first fairway. Imagine that you are playing a shot on the first hole of the course, pick a target, and select the club you will use. Visualize the shot, take a practice swing, and go through your regular alignment and setup procedure. Go through your entire routine with the same intensity you wish to maintain on the course.

KEYS TO A PUTTING WARM-UP

The most neglected part of warm-up is a putting warm-up. In fact, many players skip this part of the preround warm-up altogether. Later, they don't understand why they three-putted the first two greens. Keep in mind that putting accounts for more than 40 percent of all shots hit on the course, and take this statistic into consideration when structuring your warm-up. Tour pros would never play a competitive round without warming up on the practice green.

The goals of the putting warm-up are similar to those of the full-shot warm-up: to focus your mind, to instill confidence, and to hone your touch and feel for the speed of the greens.

The warm-up is the time to gain confidence and confirm your ability to make putts. To give yourself the best chance to putt well, you want to feel you are ready to make putts and not just wish them into the hole. More than anything else in the putting warm-up, I want players to test and gain a strong feel for the putting greens, since the speed, grain, and slope of greens are different on every course. Even the speed of the greens on your home course can change each day, depending on how the greens were cut and the weather conditions.

A big challenge when you play a new course is to adjust your touch to the unfamiliar greens. Even touring pros struggle with this: when players on the PGA and LPGA Tours play on West Coast courses (with bent-grass greens) one week and then on Southeast courses (Bermuda grass greens) the following week, they must quickly adjust to the different types of greens if they want to contend. If you can't play a practice round on the new course, your pre-round warm-up may be the only time you have to adjust your touch and feel the speed and break of the greens. But be aware that the speed of the practice green may not always match what you find on the course.

It takes only 10 to 15 minutes for a thorough putting warm-up. If you already have an established preround putting routine, that's great. If you don't, I encourage you to start today, because such a routine allows you to plan how much time you need. If you arrive late and have only 20 minutes to prepare, I recommend you spend 15 minutes on the putting green and use the remaining time for stretching and taking a few practice swings.

If you have plenty of time to get ready and always arrive at the course before your playing partners, don't tax your body and mind by spending an hour on the putting green. More putting during warm-up is not always better. You want to get focused, but not tax your concentration. A warm-up that is too long can drain your energy and hurt your focus on the course. Save your best for the course.

I teach a putting warm-up routine to my students. It includes five elements: hit some solid putts, generate a feel for the speed of the greens, instill success by making some putts, click in your focus, and rehearse your preputt routine. If you can work these elements into your putting warm-up, you will be ready to make putts. Let's discuss each of these elements separately.

HIT THE BALL SOLIDLY

One of the first feelings you want to ingrain into your mind is hitting the ball solidly on the sweet spot of the putter. This is important, because how solidly you hit your putts determines the quality of the roll of the ball. A putt that is struck solidly rolls well and gives you better speed control. Start the warm-up without a target in mind. Just hit three or four putts across the length of the green. Focus on making solid contact, staying still, and getting the ball to roll well.

Don't worry about putting to a specific target yet; you will have plenty of time to do that.

GET A FEEL FOR THE SPEED OF THE GREENS

The most important element of a putting warm-up is tuning up your feel for the speed of the greens. The ability to control pace and lag the ball close from longer distances is critical to good putting. Most three- and four-putts are caused by a lack of touch or a failure to gauge the speed of the green well. You can't develop touch in 15 minutes, but you can judge the speed of the greens better in that amount of time. The best way to judge the speed of the greens is to hit several long putts at various targets—30-, 40-, and 50-footers. I suggest hitting three putts to the opposite side of the green, trying to nudge the ball against the fringe. Match the effort of the stroke with the length of the putt. Watch the ball carefully. Does it keep rolling and rolling, or does it stop quickly? Does it turn abruptly as it slows on a sloped green, or does it stay straight? Ingrain the vision of these putts in your mind for later recall on the course. Repeat the process with both uphill and downhill putts. Hit a total of 12 putts, focusing on speed more than target. You can also adapt one or two of the drills for developing touch that I gave you in Chapter Four for use in the putting warm-up.

Next, pick out three different holes at distances of 30, 40, and 50 feet. If the green is too crowded, use tees. See how close you can putt the ball to the hole. You may not have any 50-footers on the course, but that is the best way to sense the speed and to adjust your touch. Hit long putts both downhill and uphill. Next, hit several long, breaking putts to give you a sense of how much your ball breaks on the green. Hit right-to-left and left-to-right putts, with big and small breaks. Carefully watch how each putt breaks on the green. You are not necessarily trying to make putts here (though it's great if you do). Instead, you are calibrating your feel for the greens.

INSTILL SUCCESS IN WARM-UP

Confidence erodes when you miss putts on the practice green. What do many players do first when they get on the practice green? They drop down three balls from 10 to 20 feet and miss putts! I want you to start and finish the warm-up with positive images of putts going into the hole. You should see, feel, and hear the balls go into the cup—which will fill your mind with positive images before you tee off. This will give you a feeling of comfort and confidence when you get on the first green.

After you warm up your touch, hit two- to three-foot putts only. This should be the first time in the warm-up that you are trying to make putts. Make sure you see, hear, and feel the balls go into the hole. Each putt builds a fresh image in your mind that will help your confidence on your first actual putt of the day.

CLICK IN YOUR FOCUS

The putting warm-up should be used to get your putting-game focus ready. Now is the time to focus on your performance and what you need to do to putt your best. To eliminate distractions, narrow your focus to your performance cues for making putts: reading the green, picking your line, and visualizing the ball rolling along your line and into the cup.

Start now and click in your focus. Most important, focus on the process of execution. By that I mean not mechanics, but keeping your mind locked into the process of making putts. You don't want to get ahead of yourself and think about making or missing putts when you get on the course.

REHEARSE YOUR PREPUTT ROUTINE

How often do you use your full preputt routine when you practice putting? You play on the course with your full routine, so you should use your preputt routine on the practice green. Make sure you hit your last three or four putts using your full preputt routine. Hit at least three different putts—short, long, and medium length. With each putt, keep the same pace or flow to the routine. Don't take more or less time with longer putts. Focus on seeing a line, judging the speed, and staying committed to the line. This way, you will be ready to get into your routine on the first green.

And don't be afraid to sink putts on the practice green. Some players think that making putts on the practice green wastes them, as though there will then be a shortage of putts on the course. Don't worry: if you make putts on the practice green, it's a sign of good things to come.

KEEP IT SIMPLE

Remember that the putting warm-up is only a tune-up for what's to follow, it's not practice. If you haven't putted well recently, it's hard not to try to adjust your stroke—but doing so makes you think about too many things. Work on your stroke after the round or on the days when you are not playing. You must believe you can make putts with whatever stroke you have. If you simply *must* make a change, check your fundamentals and adjust your stance or ball position only. Your best course of action is to hit several short putts to instill confidence.

YOU DON'T HAVE TO WIN WARM-UPS

Fortunately, you don't need to win warm-ups. If you're not making long putts during warm-up, don't worry. Your concentration has not peaked yet. Know that you will focus better on the course. Remember: a warm-up is just a warm-up, it's not a competition. Don't count how many putts you make or miss during your warm-up. If you don't like missing in warm-up, don't hit the ball to a cup. Instead, use tees as your target and work on fine-tuning your touch.

KEYS TO A SHORT-GAME WARM-UP

Each course you play is different from the last. How a course is designed and the length of the roughs dictate your practice before the round. If the course has a lot of bunkers, you should spend a few minutes in the sand feeling the depth and consistency of the sand. If the course has high rough around the greens, your time would be well spent hitting some chip shots around the practice green with a high-lofted club. If all the greens are elevated and well protected by bunkers, you would be wise to hit some flop shots in your warm-up. In short, evaluate the course and determine what shots you will need to hit. Then practice those shots.

TEST THE LENGTH OF THE ROUGH

Around the greens, you want to be able to predict how well the ball will come out of the rough and how much it will roll once it hits the green. Distance control is of paramount importance in chipping. To control your distance, you have to be able to gauge the amount of loft and roll you will need to get the ball close to the pin. Hit many different types of shots, preferably the ones you will have to hit most often on the course when you miss a green. Using a high-lofted wedge, hit a few lob shots from the rough around the practice green. Also hit a few running shots with a less lofted club. Remember, the key is to be able to feel and predict how the ball comes out of the rough and how it reacts once it lands on the green. On very hard greens, a ball will release and roll farther than it would on a softer green. The hardness of the greens will influence your shot and target selection when you are chipping.

TUNE UP YOUR VISUALIZATION

Again, this is not the best time to focus on technique. Instead, focus on creativity. With any chip, you have to make a judgment about the best club to use, how much loft you need, and the amount of roll required to get the ball close. You must use your imagination to see the result you want to achieve. Many players, when they get to their ball beside the green, see a shot that fits their ability and preference. This is called a first instinct, and it is usually the best shot for you to hit. You might see a high-lofted shot at first, for example. Visualize the amount of loft and roll the shot requires. Then decide on the club you need. Pick a spot or target to land the ball, and visualize the shot. You might want to play the shot both ways if you have that option, hitting a low runner and a flop shot.

GET A FEEL FOR THE SAND

Use the practice bunker, if your course has one, to test the sand. Practicing your bunker shots can give you added confidence on the first bunker shot of the day. Hit 10 to 15 shots with your sand wedge to get a feel for the texture and depth of the sand. If the sand is heavy, you will have to make a more aggressive swing. Change the speed and the length of your swing, depending on the type and depth of the sand. Vary the length of your shots: hit some short shots, the ball landing just a few feet on the green, and a few longer sand blasts. Plug a couple of balls in the sand and hit them out. The idea is to prepare for any shot you might be required to hit on the course. If the course has a lot of greenside bunkers, spend more time in the sand than usual.

GO EARLY TO THE TEE AND RELAX!

Don't wait until the last minute to go to the tee. Use the last 10 minutes of your routine to calmly walk to the tee. This is a good time to check the number of clubs and balls in your bag. Many tour pros use this time to mark their balls for easy identification of a ball in the rough or next to another ball of the same make.

After your equipment check, you have several options in the last few minutes. This can be a challenging time for many golfers who get nervous on the first tee. Butterflies are OK, as long as you get them to fly in formation. It's a sign that you are ready to play and that your body is up to the task. Don't let a simple case of first-tee butterflies turn into outright anxiety and fear.

This is not the time to start doubting yourself or your ability with thoughts like "What if I top my first shot or hit it in the trees?" This type of thinking will only make you become tense. If anything, you want to have a few positive thoughts at this time. Be confident— now is not the time to entertain doubt. Tell yourself you have paid your dues. Tell yourself you are hitting the ball well and putting well. Don't focus on score; just think about the first hole or the first shot.

Many players like to visualize exactly how they will play the first hole. See yourself hitting a good shot down the center to your target. Then imagine playing your second shot into the green. Another option is to focus on getting relaxed and calming the first-tee jitters. Breathing exercises, stretching, and visualizing yourself playing relaxed are all effective ways to do this. I feel abdominal breathing works best. Here the goal is to breathe completely through your abdominal cavity, not just through your chest. Inhale on a count of six, pause, and then exhale on a count of six. Focus on the exhalation phase of the breath—this is when your muscles are most relaxed. Maintain your focus on your breathing and let other distractions pass.

Another option is to rehearse your game plan for the round. Think about the goals you set for the day. Imagine yourself working your goals, playing one shot at a time, and focusing on the process. Recall the clubs you plan to hit on the first couple of holes. Occupy your mind with a few positive images or thoughts at this time. Some players prefer to take their mind off golf the last few minutes before teeing off. This can be a time for you to relax and talk to your playing partners. There is a benefit to this approach for players who overthink the first tee shot.

If you are already loose, keep your driver in your bag until it's your turn to play. You don't want to fiddle with your swing and get mechanical now. When it's your turn, take a couple of extra practice swings and get into your routine. If your tee time is delayed when you get to the first tee and your routine is thrown off schedule, don't panic. Use the extra time to review your game plan and rehearse your strategy for each hole. This is another good time to talk with playing partners.

A TOUR PRO WARM-UP: MARK O'MEARA'S ONE-HOUR ROUTINE

Arrive at the Golf Course (5 minutes)

Mark changes into his golf shoes in the locker room and does some preliminary stretching. He rounds up his caddie and gets his golf bag, then heads to the putting green.

Feel the Speed of the Greens (7 minutes)

Mark first hits longer putts, from 20 to 30 feet. He uses only two balls to practice distance control instead of three or more. His main focus is on hitting both putts the same distance.

Stretch to Loosen Up (5 minutes)

Mark likes to stretch a little at home before arriving at the course. Then, on the range, he swings two heavy irons slowly to loosen up his golf muscles.

Hit Some High Lobs and Low Chips (8 minutes)

Mark then hits six lob shots from the rough around the practice green. After that he hits some "bump-and-run" shots with a pitching wedge to a 7-iron. His main focus is to get a feel for how the ball will react once it lands on the green.

Test the Sand in the Bunkers (5 minutes)

Mark likes to hit 10 or 12 shots with his sand wedge to get a feel for the texture and depth of the sand. He makes a more aggressive swing in wet, heavy sand. He hits some short, medium, and long shots.

Focus on a Target (13 minutes)

Mark likes to aim at a target and see how well he controls his distance with each shot. He's also feeling his swing tendency for the day. He begins with 10 shots with a sand wedge, using half swings first and working to full swings. He varies the clubs he hits each day: One day he hits six to eight balls with odd-numbered irons. The next day he hits even irons. He is big on tempo and swinging smoothly on the range.

Hit a Few Solid Drivers (7 minutes)

Mark hits 10 to 15 balls with his driver, swinging at 85 percent of his full power. His focus is on making solid contact with each shot and sweeping the ball off the tee.

Fine-Tune Putting Touch (5 minutes)

Mark finishes the warm-up with a few putts before walking to the first tee. He mixes it up and hits some downhill, uphill, and breaking putts. He'll also hit some shorter putts from 3–5 feet.

Arrive Ahead of Tee Time (5 minutes)

Mark likes to arrive at the first tee at least five minutes early. Here he checks his clubs and balls, then makes sure he has a ball marker and glove ready to go. He also checks that he has packed a rain suit and umbrella. His goal is to be fully prepared for any playing conditions.

FINAL THOUGHTS

Don't panic if you feel nervous or get the first-tee jitters. Feeling butterflies is normal in tournament golf, especially on the first hole or two. In fact, many tour pros *want* to feel a little nervous on the first tee box, and worry if they don't. Nervousness is your body announcing that you are ready to play. The added energy can help you focus on your first few shots.

CHAPTER ELEVEN

STAYING COMMITTED
TO YOUR TRAINING
PROGRAM

Do you sometimes feel that even though you are working harder than ever before, your game simply doesn't improve? You might be feeling stronger and hitting the ball more consistently, but your scores simply have not gotten any lower. "I'm practicing more than ever, but I don't seem to be shooting better scores," many players say in frustration. The first thing I say to such a player is that to play well, you have to do more than just hit the ball well. Refining the elements of scoring—putting, chipping, sand play, course management, and mental toughness—is the key to shooting low numbers.

Second, as you advance from one level to the next—from a 10- to a 5-handicap, for example—it becomes harder and harder to improve your performance. A beginner can see daily improvements from practice, whereas a 5-handicap player's gains occur more slowly and are less detectable. This can be very frustrating for a player who feels fit, is injury-free, and is hitting the ball consistently well. If the performance plateau remains for weeks or months, a player can get easily discouraged. This is when patience, commitment, and dedication to your goals are so important: You must have the patience to wait for your hard work to pay off. You must stay committed to improving your game on a daily basis. And you must be dedicated to the goals you set for your game.

The ultimate payoff is playing better golf in tournament rounds. The purpose of your hard work and practice is to play better, not become a better practice player. Practice players make beautiful swings, hit the ball well on the practice range, and have tons of what I call practice confidence, but they lack the confidence and mental skills to play their best on the course. And that's what golf is all about: getting the most out of your ability and skills when you play. To play golf to your full potential, you must go beyond hard work and practice, and believe you can score when it counts.

USING GOALS TO STAY COMMITTED

Part of staying committed to your training program is keeping track of your progress by setting, evaluating, and reformulating your goals. The best way to do this is to set performance goals for play, practice goals, mental goals, and fitness goals. Monitoring your playing and practice goals helps you to stay focused on your practice plan and what you need to accomplish. Here are some areas for goal setting:

- Performance statistics: greens hit in regulation, fairways hit, up-and-down percentage, etc.
- Practice goals: time per week, quality of practice, golf lessons, etc.
- Mental game goals: confidence, focus, trust, composure, preshot routine, etc.
- Playing injury-free golf: overuse injuries, sprains, chronic conditions, etc.
- Physical fitness goals: strength, flexibility, stamina, etc.
- Nutrition goals: on-course nutrition and fluid intake, off-course nutrition program, diet goals, etc.

- Course management goals: study of the course, pick targets, clubs of tees, game plan, etc.
- Warm-up routine: full game, short game, putting, visualization, etc.

Goals can be divided into long-term and short-term goals. Long-term goals are those you want to accomplish by some point in the distant future: by the end of the golf season, or maybe 10 months down the road. Some examples of long-term goals are reducing your handicap by two strokes, winning an amateur event, winning the club championship, and qualifying to play on one of the tours. Make your goals specific, measurable, and time-dependent. Instead of setting the goal "to get better this year," be more specific and have a timetable in mind, such as "I want to improve my handicap three strokes by October 1 of this year."

Short-term goals are those you want to accomplish today, this week, or this month. These goals can be set for practice, competition, or personal improvement (i.e., fitness and nutrition). Examples of practice goals are making 20 putts into a row from three feet, chipping a ball into the hole from 20 feet using 10 balls, or playing nine holes every day. Examples of competition goals are hitting 10 or 14 fairways, averaging fewer than 30 putts per round, or a top 10 finish in a tournament.

Begin by setting goals for playing rounds and competition. I've taken the liberty of making a record of progress in several performance statistics (see pages 183–184), which you can modify to reflect your goals. For example, let's say you want to improve your driving performance. A good measure is fairways hit. Let's say you are hitting only five fairways. Your goal may be to average 10 fairways a round in six months.

Performance statistics are also a good gauge for measuring your strengths and weaknesses. This information can be used to structure your practice so that you spend enough time on your weak areas. Setting performance goals is also important for the following reasons:

1. to help you stay focused on what to accomplish
2. to enhance motivation and commitment

3. to assess strengths and weaknesses and structure practice accordingly

4. to see how much progress is being made

Performance statistics are easily measured and recorded during and/or after the round. To record your statistics, you can use a scorecard during the round or the Record of Progress after the round. The most commonly recorded statistics are fairways and greens hit in regulation, total putts per round, sand saves, up-and-down percentage, and birdies per round. You can record many other performance statistics, but I don't want you to make it too complicated and get lost in statistics. Pick two or three stats to focus on and record during the round, and record the others after the round. Use a journal, the Record of Progress, or a computer program to record performance statistics.

Setting and keeping track of mental-game goals is also important, although more subjective. In the Record of Progress, I've included three important areas to monitor: how well you focus on the execution of each shot, level of emotional control, and sticking to your preshot routine. These goals change depending on a person's strengths and weaknesses. You can modify the Record of Progress and use the goals that are most relevant for you. For example, maybe having fun and forgetting about score is a more appropriate goal for you at this time.

Here are some other mental-game goals:

1. Stay patient with self when mistakes are made.
2. Visualize or feel every shot before addressing the ball.
3. On every putt, commit to a line before you address the ball.
4. Pick a target on every shot that is visually obvious.
5. Focus on performance goals, not score.

Next, you should rate your strength and stamina after every round, using a scale from 1 to 10. This should be based on the following questions: Did you feel strong and finish the round with plenty of energy? Did your legs get tired at the end of the round? Did a loss of energy cause a decrease in concentration? Also set goals for your on-course nutrition and record how well you are doing on the Record of

RECORD OF PROGRESS

Statistics for round	Round 1	Round 2	Round 3	Round 4	Round 5	Round 6	Round 7	Round 8	Round 9
Date:									
Course played									
Fairways hit (total)									
Greens hit (total)									
Putts per round (total)									
Birdies per round									
Sand save percent									
Up-and-down percent									
Execution focus (1–10)									

(Continued)

RECORD OF PROGRESS (*Continued*)

Statistics for round	Round 1	Round 2	Round 3	Round 4	Round 5	Round 6	Round 7	Round 8	Round 9
Emotional control (Y/N)									
Preshot routine (%)									
Strength and endurance (1–10)									
On-course nutrition (P/F/G/E)									
Course preparation (P/F/G/E)									
Game plan (P/F/G/E)									
Proper warm-up routine (Y/N)									

Progress. Did you follow your on-course nutritional plan? This should include the amount of fluids you consumed during the round.

Set goals for course preparation, game plan, and warm-up routine. Did you study the course, check yardage plates or trees, and pick targets off the tees? Did you develop a game plan with this information? How well did you follow the game plan you set before the round? Lastly, did you complete your full warm-up routine? Were you confident and focused before you got to the first tee?

AVOID BURNOUT

It's easy to overdo anything in life, especially if you are a perfectionist. The goal of this book is not to make you a great practice player but to help you play better and win through better practice and more complete preparation. Perfectionistic players live for what has been presented in this book, because it gives them more tasks to master. Always remember that the best practice matches the mind-set of and challenges found in tournament golf.

You can burn out on golf, a game you love, by overworking yourself in your attempt to lower your scores. At times you need to rest and smell the roses along the path to your dreams. All work and no fun makes golf a dull game. Once a week, take a day off from golf—both you and your family will appreciate it. If you've played tournaments for more than four weeks in a row, it's time to rest and recover. Take a week off. You will come back refreshed and excited to play again.

FINAL THOUGHTS

Now you have the building blocks for a total training program. I hope by now you see the importance of a well-rounded training program to competing at any level. I also hope you see that for the program to be of any benefit you must honestly evaluate your strengths and weaknesses and chart out a journey toward playing better golf. It's easy to practice your strengths and ignore the weak parts of your game. The hard part is having the discipline to work on your game's deficiencies as well as the areas you enjoy.

I always tell my clients that to improve a golfer must do three things. First, he must learn skills (a method, technique, or strategy) that can be applied to his game. But this knowledge alone is not enough. Second, the player must apply the new knowledge and skills to his game by practicing daily. But improvement is still far away. To complete the process, a player must commit to getting better each and every day, day after day, week after week, month after month. Without all three elements—learning, practice, and commitment— improvement cannot occur. Learn from the best, practice in the most effective way, and stay committed to the process of getting better every day.

How do you stay committed to your practice plan and achieving your goals? By reminding yourself each and every day of your dreams and doing the daily tasks needed to reach your goals. And don't forget to enjoy the ride along the way. The process of striving for goals and enjoying each moment is what life is all about. Life is fulfilling when we immerse ourselves every day in the process of achieving our goals through our own motivation, wisdom, and knowledge.

CHAPTER TWELVE

TOURNAMENT PREP RX: DOC COHN ANSWERS YOUR QUESTIONS

You have learned how to get more from your golf lessons, how to practice with a mission, and how to prepare your mind and body for tournament play. You have learned everything from better course management to developing a preround warm-up routine that helps you play better. You have the tools and knowledge to get started on your way to winning golf. Now I want to respond to some questions I'm often asked about practice and preparation in these different areas. In this chapter, I present answers to both these questions and to some that golfers should ask me, but don't.

I have only two hours a day to practice. If my practice time is limited, what should I work on to play my best?

It doesn't matter if you practice 30 hours or two hours a week—your practice needs to be quality practice (refer to Chapter Four). What you should practice if you have only two hours depends on the current state of your game and what you most need to improve. First, assess the performance of each area of your game (driving, iron play, putting, chipping, sand play, etc.). What areas of your game need the most improvement? Look at your performance in areas such as fairways hit, greens hit in regulation, total putts, sand save percentage, up-and-down percentage, and number of birdies, pars, and bogeys. Statistics don't lie, but be aware that some are misleading. Total putts per round does not accurately reflect your putting performance, for example. If you average hitting 13 greens a round but take 34 putts, that is a good indication you need to improve your putting. But if you hit 18 greens and take 34 putts, that may not reflect your putting performance. Remember that working on your short game is the fastest way to lower your scores.

Don't interpret this as meaning that I want you to spend those two hours working on your putting only. If you have the facilities, you should practice all parts of your game. As a guideline, at least half of your time should be devoted to your short game—putting, chipping, pitching, and sand shots. The other half should be devoted to long-game and specialty shots. If you have a weakness in your game, such as putting, spend an extra 15 minutes a day practicing that part of your game.

Use the same approach if you have only an hour to practice. Spend a few minutes each day with each part of your game. Do 15 minutes of putting, 15 minutes of chipping and bunker play, and 30 minutes of full game practice. Research on motor learning indicates that you learn and perform better if you work on all parts of your game in one practice session. In other words, don't hit drivers for an hour on Monday and then practice only putting the next day. Spread it around each time you practice.

I'm learning to swing differently right now with my new instructor. How long will it take for me to learn the new swing, and how often do I need to practice to ingrain it?

Playing golf when you are "between" two swings can be a challenge. What I mean by this is that the swing changes you are working on have not been ingrained, or learned enough, so that the new swing can replace the old swing. Under pressure, golfers revert to their dominant habits, which in this case is usually the last ingrained swing. This can lead to inconsistent play, a decrease in confidence, and a lot of frustration.

When you make major changes in your swing, your confidence may decline temporarily because the quality and consistency of your performance declines. You may find that your performance declines in tournaments even when you are practicing more than ever. The changes have not produced reliable and repeatable results, and this can be frustrating. This is why it is best to make swing changes in the off-season or at another time outside of tournament season. You may want to cut back on tournament play at this time until your confidence improves. As performance improves, so will your confidence.

You have to be patient in waiting for your new swing to become ingrained. It has to become the dominant habit. Many players don't understand how long it takes to make a major swing change. The problem is that you have to extinguish the old swing and replace it with the new one. Some experts say it takes several repetitions a day for 60 days to ingrain a new habit.

If you practice every day, you can expect the change to become ingrained in two to three months, provided you are practicing correctly and with the appropriate feedback. Of course, this also depends on your present skill level and your innate ability. If you can't practice every day or if you are not making the proper swing every time, it will take longer to ingrain the new swing. Remember that if you practice the wrong move, you just get good at the wrong move. Make sure you are practicing the right move: use correct feedback and check in with your instructor at least two times a month.

When I make a swing change, my short game or some other facet of my game goes into the tank. This happens even if I continue to practice the other aspects of my game. How can I overcome this problem?

Most golfers get too caught up in developing a perfect swing, often at the expense of their short game. They feel this is the best way to lower scores. Usually, when a player has this attitude and works hard on his swing, other parts of his game suffer. This is why a practice plan is so important.

Don't let yourself get distracted by the "perfect golf swing" mentality. Emphasize your putting and chipping just as much as your full golf swing. As a guideline, make sure you practice your short game as much as—if not more than—your full golf swing. Putting accounts for 40 percent or more of your total score, but I bet you don't spend 40 percent of your practice time on putting. A golfer may think: "When I can hit the ball well enough, I will begin to work on my short game." Then this golfer may have three or four three-putts in the next round and wonder why he isn't scoring better.

I don't seem to be shooting better scores after taking several lessons. How do I know if I'm making progress with the swing changes and the instructor is doing a good job?

You have to remember that hitting balls on the range or making putts on the practice green does not necessarily result in shooting low numbers. Other factors, such as course management, your mental game, and your ability to score, are just as important as the ability to hit a good shot on the range. One way to know if you are improving is to assess the consistency of your shots on and off the course. Are your shots more consistent from day to day or even from one shot to the next? Also, are your statistics, such as the number of greens hit per round, improving? Your swing may be improving but not yet paid off on the course, because you have not put it all together to score your best. Scoring is the name of the game.

Now it's a matter of playing golf and scoring well. This means simply getting the job done and not worrying about how. Your goal now is to put the lessons and hours of practice to work when you play. Your scoring game is the best asset you have. After working hard on your swing, you may have neglected the short game. It may be time to make the switch to working on your short game and your scoring shots, such as wedge play, bunker play, chipping, and putting.

I often skip breakfast before I play. What's the best meal to eat before I play golf if I'm in a big hurry to get to the course?

You don't want to skip the most important meal of the day, especially if it's your only meal before you play. When you play on an empty stomach, your body must pull energy from its fat reserves. The body functions best when it has readily available energy for fuel, so it is important to eat a balanced meal that includes carbohydrates, protein, and fat. Carbohydrates provide readily usable fuel. Protein helps to rebuild muscle tissue. And fat helps you feel satiated for longer. Refer to Chapter Eight to find out what foods are the best sources of carbohydrates, protein, and fat.

I fear that working out with weights may cause my muscles to get too large and thus inefficient for golf. Can my muscles get too big from working out and interfere with my swing?

The goal of an exercise program is to improve strength, flexibility, and stamina. A larger muscle is a stronger muscle, but that doesn't mean it's more flexible. Your exercise trainer should have you on a program that helps you become more flexible as you gain muscle strength. You *can* develop muscles that interfere with your golf swing, but to do so you would have to work out with weights for two hours a day while doing many sets and keeping the repetitions per set very low. If you keep your repetitions per set above 15, you shouldn't have a problem with developing muscles that are too big for golf, especially if you work on flexibility training at the same time.

Make sure to balance your workout by including aerobic exercise, flexibility training, and weight training. Aerobic, or heart and lung, exercise is the best type of training; it improves your stamina and gives you extra energy for those closing holes.

In the off-season during winter, my game gets rusty and it takes me a couple of months to get back to form in the spring. What's the best way to prepare my game for the start of the golf season so I don't feel like I'm starting all over again?

Does it take you two to three months to get back to midsummer form? A break from golf is great, because you can return with a fresh attitude and a clear mind. I know this because I grew up in Buffalo, New York, where the winters are long and cold. The trick is to keep your game sharp during the months off so you can play as well as you did in the fall. Many urban areas in cold climates have indoor practice facilities to help golfers stay in form over the winter.

You can do some other things to keep your golf game sharp in the off-season. This is when you need to be creative with practice and have the discipline and commitment to work on other areas of your training program. This is also a great time to start a fitness program or work with a personal trainer so you can be as fit as possible when the season starts. During this time you can also work on your mental preparation (refer to Chapter Five), perhaps by reading books and listening to tapes that help keep you motivated.

Jack Nicklaus said that if you can't hit balls on the range, the next best option is to swing a club indoors. He used to take one hundred swings a day to keep the rust off when he couldn't practice or didn't have time to. Use a mirror when you practice indoors. Many players do this to check positions of the club during their swing.

Use this time to work on your putting. I don't know many pros who don't practice putting indoors when they are home. You can set up a putting course indoors at home if you have a smooth and fast carpet. If you don't have this type of carpet, you can buy a strip of indoor/outdoor carpet or purchase a good putting track.

There are several types of indoor putting tracks you can buy from golf stores. You can also practice chipping balls indoors if you are creative—that is, if your spouse will put up with it.

Use imagery to help you stay tuned up mentally. Many gymnasts use visualization to stay sharp when they are sidelined by an injury or are too tired to practice. You can use imagery or visualization to play a round of golf, mentally practice your golf swing, or to correct an error in your swing.

A study was conducted on the effectiveness of imagery on basketball players' foul-shooting performance. Three groups participated in the study. One group physically practiced foul shots, another group imagined shooting foul shots, and a third group did nothing. The group that just visualized shooting foul shots performed just as well as the group that did physical practice only. And they both performed better than the control group.

Remember your goals for your golf game. What can you do in the off-season to help you reach these goals? You may not be able to play golf in the winter, but you can do a lot of other things that will pay off when you start playing in the spring.

I get bored when I practice for more than three hours at one time, and then I lose focus. What can I do to stay focused and sharp when I practice for long periods of time?

Keeping practice interesting is a big challenge for professional players, who may spend as much as eight hours a day practicing and playing. When you feel bored, that means you don't feel challenged enough, and this causes your focus to decrease.

If you become bored, first take a 30-minute break to relax and clear your mind. Put down the clubs and have something to eat or drink.

The key is to keep practice interesting and exciting. This is where practice goals are important. Use goals to challenge yourself on the range or practice green. For example, you can challenge yourself to hit 10 or 14 fairways on the range. Imagine a fairway in the driving range and see if you can hit it on 10 or 14 tries. Play 18 holes on the range. If you hit driver and 5-iron on the first hole of your home course, hit driver and 5-iron on the range. Then play the next hole the same way. The more "games" you can play to make practice interesting, the better. Reward yourself for meeting your practice goals.

Creating competition is another great way to keep the fun and excitement in practice. Have a putting contest with a friend or playing partner on the practice green. Play 18 holes on the practice green. Be creative with your practice, and challenge yourself.

Next time you lose focus, try the "two-minute drill." The goal of this drill is to focus your attention on practice for just two minutes. See how keenly you can focus for that duration. When the two-minute period is over, you can relax. Short bursts of intense focus with periods of rest or inactivity are better than practicing with 50 percent focus for the entire practice. Eventually, you will find that you can stretch this drill out to four or five minutes.

How should I prepare my mind the night before a tournament so I can play my best?

You have two options. The first is to take your mind off golf and just have fun. Forget about golf. Go out with your family, see a movie, or read a book. There are certain benefits to taking your mind off golf and relaxing. First, you will have more fun. Second, you won't stress out about the next day's round. Third, it may be easier to get to sleep, especially if you are the type of person who worries about the next day's round.

If you are playing in a tournament and have a lead in the event going into the last round, it's helpful to do your normal routine. Don't sit home and visualize the next round if you normally would go out. You want to feel fresh and ready to go.

Your second option is to focus on the next day's game plan. If you decide to do this, you may want to go over each hole in your mind. Think about the clubs you will hit off each tee, what targets you have selected in the practice round, and where you want to place your shots on the green.

You can also visualize the next day's round. You can imagine playing the course just as you would want to. But match your visualization to your ability level. If you normally hit your driver 250 yards and a 5-iron to the green, it's not realistic to imagine hitting a 300-yard drive and a wedge to the green. See yourself playing with total confidence and composure. If you hit a bad shot in your imagery, replay the shot.

I find it hard to get focused when I play practice rounds. I need to bet with others to get into the round. Is this wrong?

You are not alone. Many players have trouble getting up for a round that doesn't mean anything or if scores don't need to be posted. The lack of excitement or interest during the round hurts their focus and intensity. You are the type of player who gets excited to play only when you're in a tournament situation; the excitement and intensity of the event brings up your level of concentration.

Anything you can do to get focused for a practice round will be helpful. A small wager is OK, but I prefer that you set a few goals for the practice round instead. For example, challenge yourself to hit as many fairways as you can. Play the round for a score. You don't have to win the round, but you do want to be focused enough that you can do a good job of studying the course and developing a smart game plan. The goal is to use the practice round to prepare yourself to play the course to the best of your ability when the tournament starts.

I love to practice golf. I prefer practicing to playing. I wonder sometimes if I practice too much. Is that possible?

It's great that you love to practice, but it *is* possible to practice too much. To improve, you have to train a lot and train the right way, as I have discussed. It seems you have plenty of motivation to train and improve. But often I see players who get too comfortable with practice. These players are stuck in a training mentality. They are most confident on the range or practice green.

When they play, they don't feel as comfortable because they have not developed playing confidence.

If this sounds like you, back off on the amount of practice you do and start to play more. A good rule is to play as much as you practice. Too much practice, especially beating balls on the range, can also cause you to become stale and burn out. It's hard to be fresh and excited about golf if you practice so much that you are tired and drained before you play in a tournament. You can also become more prone to overuse injuries. Hitting so many balls that your wrist becomes sore is not a good way to prepare to play your best in a tournament.

A good alternative is to practice different shots on the course. This may require that you play in the early morning or late afternoon, when the course is not crowded and you can play a few different shots per hole. Use simulation training on the course: Hit a drive and then pick it up. Play a shot from a distance that is giving you trouble, hit a shot around a tree, or hit a shot from a lie that's a trouble spot. Practice your distance control by using a wedge or two from different distances. Hit a few difficult chips or sand shots around the greens. This type of practice is more creative and specific to the shots you will need to hit in tournaments. It forces you to hit all the shots.

If you spend every day on the range and the practice green without much competitive play, you probably practice too much. If you have a nagging injury from hitting too many balls, you probably practice too much. If you like to practice more than play, you practice too much.

I can't decide on one putter to use. I practice with several different putters and then decide which putter to put in the bag just before the next tournament. Am I hurting my chances to putt my best?

Searching for a perfect putter is a red flag to me. Great putters carry only one putter with them—for example, Ben Crenshaw and his "Little Ben." When I see a player searching for the right putter or driver, I know he is lacking confidence in that area. Usually the player uses in the tournament whatever is working well that week in practice.

A good golfer can putt with any putter. He has confidence in his ability to putt and doesn't rely on a magic wand to make putts for him. I urge you to use the same putter in practice that you will use in tournaments. Every putter has a different feel and look to it. It's best to feel comfortable with the club you will use in competition. Don't switch back and forth between several putters. That's just using your equipment as a crutch for putting woes.

I become very tense the morning before I play a tournament. I start to worry about everything that can go wrong. Sometimes I can't even eat. What can I do to relax before I go to the course and while I warm up?

It sounds as if you become pessimistic when you are nervous. You think about the tournament and about the ways you can screw up. This negative thinking makes you more tense and anxious. The feelings of anxiety make you worry even more about the tournament. It's a vicious cycle. If you can't have positive thoughts and be optimistic about the event, it's best that you don't even think about the tournament. When I hear a player making excuses for not playing well and he hasn't even played yet, I know he's in trouble.

Counter your negative thinking with optimistic thinking. This means developing a more optimistic attitude. Focus on the reasons you will succeed. Make a list of the reasons why you will play well. Then review those reasons the morning before the event. You can also blow off tension by doing some light exercise, taking a bath, or listening to music.

Develop one or two relaxation exercises to rely on when you feel anxious, such as a breathing exercise or meditation. You need to counter the anxiety mentally and physically, because it affects both your mental and physical state. Make sure you stay focused on playing well, and use physical means of relaxation as you go through your normal routine before playing.

I always find a way to sabotage myself when I play in tournaments. I'll leave a club home, I'll forget to bring my rain gear and it rains, or I arrive late to the course and can't warm up. How can I plan or prepare better so I don't get rattled when I do something dumb?

I don't think you engage in self-sabotage, but I do think you need to plan better for tournaments and prepare your mind for the unexpected so you don't get rattled when something unexpected happens. First, establish a routine for yourself the day of the tournament. Set aside time for a meal, getting to the course, warm-up routine, and a few extra minutes on the tee. Write a checklist of equipment that you will need, and remember to look at it before you leave home. Your checklist may include clubs, balls, rain gear, umbrella, snacks, and anything else you may need. Develop a similar list for things you need to do at the course before you play.

Second, anticipate anything that can go wrong. This can include something that happened in the past, such as having no rain gear with you when a hard rain started. You don't want to let a simple problem like leaving a club at home ruin your attitude and distract you for the rest of the day. Think about how you can deal with each problem in a way that won't hurt your focus and confidence. You can be ready for anything that happens by rehearsing how you will behave in that situation.

How can I peak my game for an important tournament? I practice hard before the event, but the extra practice doesn't seem to help me play better.

This is an important question for anyone who plays in a qualifying event, a club championship, or the NCAA finals. Professional golfers who play in the PGA Tour qualifying school at the end of the year want their games to be peaking at this time. I urge players to not wait until just before the tournament to practice and prepare hard. The time to begin preparation is two to three months before the event.

You shouldn't start a new exercise program, a new diet, or a new practice regimen just before the event. It's best to keep your normal routine and lifestyle in the weeks leading up to the tournament. There is often a delayed reaction to practice. The time to taper off your heavy training is when you get close to the start of the event—say, within two weeks.

This approach is similar to that taken by most long-distance runners and track athletes. Their heavy training should come weeks and months before the meet. As they get closer to the event, they gradually taper their training. This way they are in great shape and well rested for the big event, not tired, sore from training, or stale. You should apply the same approach to training for a big tournament.

Just before the tournament, shift your training to preparation for the course and working on short-game practice. What clubs will you hit most often around the greens? Will you need a sharp bunker game? Is the rough high around the greens, requiring you to practice those shots? The last few days of your preparation you should focus on studying the course, making a game plan, and tuning up the shots you will need around the greens.

You might consider trying different approaches to preparation to see what method helps you play your best. Does doing more preparation help? Or does taking a more casual approach to preparation help you play better? This takes discipline, but the effort will pay off. Keep a practice log or journal on your preparation for each round. In the journal, record your practice routine, results of practice rounds, notes about each hole, what you did the day before and the morning of each round, etc. After a few rounds with different preparation approaches, evaluate what works best for you.

I have found that for some players, less is better. Some golfers actually overprepare and overanalyze before tournaments. Their expectations get out of hand. If the tournament round doesn't go exactly as they expected, they unravel and perform poorly. Similarly, there are undermotivated players who need to step up their preparation for tournaments. These players think that preparing for a tournament simply means making sure the clubs are clean and enough golf balls are in the bag.

REFERENCES

Batt, M. E. "A Survey of Golf Injuries in Amateur Golfers." *British Journal of Sports Medicine* 26 (1): 63–65 (1992).

Ellis, A., and C. Tafrate. *How to Control Anger Before It Controls You.* Secaucus, New Jersey: Carol Publishing Group, 1997.

Farnsworth, Craig. *See It and Sink It: Mastering Putting Through Peak Visual Performance.* New York: HarperCollins, 1997.

Geisler, Paul. "PGA Tour and Senior PGA Tour Injuries Rates." Interviewed by Centinela Hospital Fitness Van Staff, 1995.

Hosea, T. M., and C. J. Gatt. "Back Pain in Golf." *Clinics in Sports Medicine: Golf Injuries.* Philadelphia: W. B. Saunders, 1996.

McCarrol, J. R., and T. S. Gioe. "Professional Golfers and the Price They Pay." *The Physician and Sports Medicine* 10 (7): 64–70 (1982).

PEAK PERFORMANCE SPORTS
MENTAL GAME LIBRARY

Great Putting—Right Now! Mental Keys to Confident Putting
Read by Dr. Patrick J. Cohn and Robert Winters, M.A., who are two leading experts in putting psychology. This tape teaches how to create a great putting attitude right away, and putt with more confidence. Great for anyone who plays, coaches, or works with golfers. Perfect for golfers who are streaky putters and those who consistently struggle with putting.
   One Audiotape. 74 minutes. $12.00. 888-742-7225 or www.peaksports.com

Make Your Most Confident Stroke: A Guide to a One-Putt Mind-set
Tour winner Grant Waite, Dr. Cohn, and other PGA Tour winners reveal the secrets of being confident and focused on the greens. They teach the characteristics that successful putters possess and how to think like a great putter. Golfers learn how to develop a focused and confident putting routine. Dr. Cohn also teaches drills for developing touch.
   Video. 37 minutes. $22.95. 888-742-7225 or www.peaksports.com

The Mental Art of Putting: Using Your Mind to Putt Your Best
Dr. Patrick J. Cohn, Ph.D., and Robert Winters, M.A., teach you how to putt with greater confidence, more focus, and less fear. Several tour pros offer insight on the mind and abilities of great putters. Golfers learn preround, warm-up, and preshot routines for great putting. This book contains everything a golfer should know about the mind-set needed to putt one's best.
   Book. 140 pages. $19.95. 888-742-7225 or www.peaksports.com

The Mental Game of Golf: A Guide to Peak Performance
The Mental Game of Golf teaches golfers how to master the mental game and play with greater confidence and composure. It combines the author's work, research, and tips from tour pros to illustrate the key mental skills and routines needed to play your best. This book is a perfect introduction to the subject for junior, college, and pro golfers.

Book. 169 pages. $19.95. 888-742-7225 or www.peaksports.com

Peak Performance Golf Insights: A Newsletter for Serious Golfers
Edited by Dr. Patrick Cohn, this newsletter teaches golfers how to focus better and play with more confidence. You learn how to apply field-tested methods in sports psychology and perspectives from tour professionals to help you develop a winning attitude.

Newsletter—Spring and Fall. One-year subscription: $12. 888-742-7225 or www.peaksports.com.

Think to Win: How to Manage Your Mind on the Golf Course
Read by Dr. Patrick J. Cohn, this unique two-tape audio program teaches golfers how to avoid self-sabotage and take their practice game to the course. The program gives field-tested practical strategies to help golfers transfer their skills to the course and play with confidence, composure, and consistency. A great introduction to the mental game of golf and how golfers sabotage themselves on the course.

Two Audiotapes. 110 minutes. $18.95. 888-742-7225 or www.peaksports.com

INDEX

ABOUT THE AUTHOR

Dr. Patrick J. Cohn heads Peak Performance Sports in Orlando, Florida. A leading sport and golf psychologist, author, and professional speaker, Dr. Cohn teaches his methods to golfers on the PGA Tour, LPGA Tour, BUY.COM Tour, and to several collegiate and amateur players. Dr. Cohn earned a Ph.D. in sports psychology from the University of Virginia in 1991. He is considered by experts in his field as the leading authority on preshot routines and putting psychology. Dr. Cohn developed his mental training program from more than a decade of work and research with elite athletes. He is the author of *The Mental Game of Golf: A Guide to Peak Performance* and coauthor of *The Mental Art of Putting: Using Your Mind to Putt Your Best*. He stars in the audio book *Think to Win: How to Manage Your Mind on the Golf Course* and the video *Make Your Most Confident Stroke: A Guide to a One-Putt Mind-set*, and costars in the audio *Great Putting—Right Now! Mental Keys to Confident Putting*. Dr. Cohn also teaches sports psychology to PGA professionals, athletic trainers, and health care professionals. His education seminars are approved for education credits by the PGA of America. He has appeared twice as a special guest on the Golf Channel, and he writes for Golfweb, *GOLF Magazine*, and PGA magazine.

Contact Dr. Cohn at:
Peak Performance Sports
7380 Sand Lake Rd., Suite 500
Orlando, Florida 32819
Phone: 407-248-9830
Toll-free: 888-742-7225
E-mail: PGAPACK@aol.com
Website: www.peaksports.com

About the Contributors

Mike Bender is ranked as one of the top 100 teaching professionals in the United States by *GOLF Magazine* and the director of instruction at Timacuan Golf Academy in Orlando, Florida. Contact Mike at 407-321-0444.

Paul Geisler, M.A., ATC/L, is president of KineticGolf and SPEC Systems, Inc. and a sports medicine and athletic training instructor in the Department of Health and Kinesiology at Georgia Southern University in Statesboro, Georgia. Contact Paul at 912-587-9833.

Karen Sue Beerbower, M.S., R.D., is the president of Nutritional Guidance, Inc., in Winter Park, Florida. Karen served as the official consultant to the 1996 Olympic Women's Soccer Team. Contact Karen at 407-741-5812.